BRINGING HOME THE SUSHI

AN INSIDE LOOK AT JAPANESE BUSINESS THROUGH JAPANESE COMICS

Bringing Home the Sushi

An Inside Look at Japanese Business through Japanese Comics

Laura K. Silverman, Editor

Mangajin, Inc.
Atlanta, Georgia

Distributed in the United States by Weatherhill, Inc.
300 Long Beach Boulevard
Stratford, Connecticut 06497-7116

Distributed in Japan by Sekai Shuppan Kenkyū Centre
2-18-9 Minami-Aoyama, Minato-ku
Tokyo 107

Published by Mangajin, Inc.
P.O. Box 7119, Marietta, Georgia 30065

Printed in the United States of America
First edition

ISBN 0-9634335-2-0 (U.S.)
ISBN 4-916079-01-9 (Japan)

Contents

Acknowledgments

The following people were indispensable to the making of this book: Vaughan Simmons and Hiromichi Moteki, who directed the project; Kazuko Ashizawa, who spent countless hours scanning and laying out pages; Lev Grote and Virginia Murray, who helped with editing, translation, typing, design, and everything else that needed doing, often on very short notice; Wayne Lammers, who provided a large portion of the translation; Mayumi Otsuka, who typed in all of the Japanese text; Ikuko Okuyama and Donna Horne, who proofread; and Peter Goodman of Stone Bridge Press and Barbara Brackett of Weatherhill, Inc., who provided much appreciated professional advice. To the many others not mentioned here whose assistance and support were generously given, I am greatly indebted.

Risu Akizuki (*OL Shinkaron*) made her debut in 1988 with *Okusama Shinkaron*. Soon after, she began serializing her most famous work, the four-frame manga *OL Shinkaron*, in *Shūkan Mōningu*. *OL Shinkaron* continues to sell widely in book form; there are nine volumes of previously serialized works, eight pocket editions of original works, and an English library edition. Other works include *Kashimashi House* and a variety of four-frame comics currently being serialized in the *Asahi Shimbun* and NHK's *Kyō no Ryōri*.

Jirō Gyū (*Eigyō Tenteko Nisshi*, writer) left high school and worked a variety of jobs before making his debut as a manga storywriter. Today he submits his manga creations from the Gangyōji Temple, where he resides as a Buddhist priest and goes by the name of Ushigome Shinkaku. Representative works include *Kugishi Sabuyan* and *Hōchōnin Ajihei*. Early in his career he was awarded Kadokawa's Yaseijidai New Writer's Award.

Kenshi Hirokane (*Ningen Kōsaten*, artist; *Kachō Shima Kōsaku*) graduated from Waseda University in 1970 and was a salaryman at Matsushita for three years before quitting to work on his manga while supporting himself as an illustrator. He made his debut one year later with *Kaze Kaoru*. He won the Shogakukan Manga Award in 1985 for *Ningen Kōsaten*, and the Kodansha Manga Award in 1991 for *Kachō Shima Kōsaku*.

Ken'ichi Kitami (*Tsuri-Baka Nisshi*, artist) went to work as an assistant for Fujio Akatsuka, the "gag manga king," after graduating from art school with a degree in photography. He made his debut with *Shōnen Kingu* and *Dojokkofunakko* in 1988 before joining forces with Jūzō Yamasaki in 1989 to produce *Tsuri-Baka Nisshi*, for which he won the Shogakukan Manga Award in 1983. Kitami also won a Japan Manga Artist Association Award in 1989 for *Yakeato no Genki-kun*.

Yōsuke Kondō (*Eigyō Tenteko Nisshi*, artist) went straight from high school to work as an assistant to Fujio Akatsuka and Ken'ichi Kitami before making his debut as a manga artist. Well-known works include *Kanshiki Kenshi* and *Kore ni Kimeta*. Currently he is serializing *Konna me Anna me* in the evening newspaper *Nikkan Gendai*.

Tatsuo Nitta (*Torishimariyaku Hira Namijirō*), an avid manga fan since his elementary school days, often contributed to boys' manga magazines in his youth. As an adult, he became a junior high school art teacher, but quit at the age of 23 to devote himself full-time to manga. His most popular manga include *Sara Nin Man* (currently running in *Big Comikku Superiōru*) and *Shizukanaru Don* (currently running in *Manga Sandē*).

Sadao Shōji (*Sarariiman Senka*) dropped out of college in his third year to pursue his dream of becoming a manga artist. He struggled in obscurity for many years before gaining recognition in 1967 for *Shin Manga Bungaku Zenshū* and *Shōji-kun*. He is the creator of numerous manga, including *Asatte-kun*, which began running in the *Mainichi*

Shimbun in 1974 and continues to run today. Shōji won the 16th Bungei Shunjū Manga Award in 1970.

Hiroshi Tanaka (*Nakuna! Tanaka-kun*) was a construction worker and an architectural designer prior to becoming a manga artist. His most popular manga other than *Nakuna! Tanaka-kun* include *Ojama-san* and *Māchi-kun*. Currently he is serializing *NG Kazoku* in the monthly *Manga Life Original*.

Kazuyoshi Torii (*Toppu wa Ore da!*) moved to Tokyo at the age of 19 to pursue his dream of becoming a manga artist. He soon found work as an animator for *Sutajio Zero* (a studio run by Fujio Akatsuka and other manga artists) and then as an assistant to Akatsuka. With Akatsuka's help, he made his debut in that same year with *Kuchinashi Inu*, and went on to publish a variety of gag manga before striking out on his own in 1970. Representative works include *Kutabare! Tōchan* and *Uwasa no Tenkai*.

Masao Yajima (*Ningen Kōsaten*, writer) is a former salaryman who decided to change careers and become a screenwriter shortly after winning two screenwriting contests in his mid-twenties. Although he has written numerous manga stories, the majority of his work has been for television. He won the Shogakukan Manga Award for *Ningen Kōsaten* in 1985.

Jūzō Yamasaki (*Tsuri-Baka Nisshi*, writer), an avid fisherman, worked for ten years as an assistant director at Tōei Television Production before a labor dispute motivated him to switch careers and become a manga storywriter. He won the Shogakukan Manga Award in 1983 for *Tsuri-Baka Nisshi* and the Kodansha Manga Award in 1985 for *Okashina Futari*.

Essayists

Bernice Cramer is a strategic management consultant who lives in Boston, Massachusetts. As president of Next Frame Inc., she counsels the leaders of both Japanese and American corporations on issues of vision, strategy, and change. She lived in Japan for 13 years.

Peter Duus is William H. Bonsall Professor of History at Stanford University. He has written extensively on the history of Japanese political parties, modern Japanese political thought, and modern Japanese imperialism, and has authored several books, including *Party Rivalry and Political Change in Taisho Japan*, *Feudalism in Japan*, and *The Rise of Modern Japan*. His current research focuses on the social history of Japan during the period of rapid economic growth in the 1950s and 1960s.

Glen S. Fukushima is vice president of the American Chamber of Commerce in Japan. From 1985 to 1990, he directed Japanese affairs at the Office of the United States Trade Representative (USTR) in Washington, D.C. A graduate of Stanford (A.B.) and Harvard

(A.M., J.D., A.B.D.), he has also studied at Keio University and Tokyo University in Japan. He is currently vice chairman of the Japan-United States Friendship Commission.

Herbert Glazer went to Japan in 1959 with the navy and returned in 1965 to teach International Business at Sophia University in Tokyo. He is currently a professor of International Business at The American University in Washington, D.C., and a visiting professor at Sophia. His main interest these days is the use of the World Wide Web as a vehicle for communication within the global enterprise.

Toshimasa Kii teaches industrial sociology and intercultural communication at Georgia State University in Atlanta, Georgia. He also consults with multinational corporations in the areas of cross-cultural business communication (Japan and the U.S.) and diversity management.

Tomofusa Kure, a graduate of the law department of Waseda University, is a critic well known in Japan for his original and penetrating views on a variety of subjects, including manga. Among the many books he has authored are *Dokushōka no Shingijutsu* ("New Techniques of the Avid Reader"), *Gendai Manga no Zentaizō* ("A Comprehensive Overview of Manga Today"), and *Chi no Shūkaku* ("The Harvesting of Wisdom").

Steve Leeper is president of Transnet, a translating and consulting company based in Hiroshima. He is also foreign liaison advisor to Hiroshima-based Molten Corporation (a manufacturer of athletic balls and industrial rubber products) and serves on the board of both Molten USA and Molten North America Corporation.

Jeannie Lo graduated from Harvard (A.B.) in 1987 and published her first book, *Office Ladies/Factory Women* (M.E. Sharpe) in 1990. After college she moved to Tokyo to work as an editor for LOOK JAPAN magazine and the *Asian Wall Street Journal*. She is currently a research associate in the cell biology group at Genetech, Inc., in San Francisco, California.

T. R. Reid is bureau chief of the *Washington Post*'s Far East Bureau, based in Tokyo, and a commentator on Japan and Asian affairs for National Public Radio's "Morning Edition." In Japan, he appears regularly on news analysis television shows such as "Za Week," "Keizai Scope," and "Asa Made Nama Terebi." He writes a regular column for *Shūkan Shinchō* magazine and occasional columns for the newspaper *Nikkan Sports*. He has also written three books in English and two in Japanese.

Mark Schilling, a resident of Tokyo since 1975, writes about sumo for *Sumo World*, Japanese films for the *Japan Times,* and the Japanese movie industry for *Screen International*. He is currently researching and writing a book on postwar Japanese popular culture.

Greg Tenhover spent eight years working as a cross-cultural management consultant in Japan and the U.S., consulting for major corporations such as Arthur Andersen, Nomura Securities, and General Electric. He is author of the book *Unlocking The Japanese Business Mind* and is currently advertising director at Mangajin, Inc.

Glossary

Geisha: Female entertainers trained in the traditional arts. *Geisha* are sometimes called in to provide refined entertainment at formal Japanese-style dinners and banquets.

Maiko: Apprentice *geisha*.

Oden: A variety of ingredients boiled for hours together in a soy sauce and kelp stock. Some typical *oden* ingredients are hard-boiled eggs, chunks of *daikon* radish, small potatoes, and blocks of tofu. *Oden* is commonly eaten in the winter and is popular as a late-night snack after drinking, usually bought and eaten at outdoor stands near train stations.

OLs (Office Ladies): the female workers who handle most of the mundane tasks of an office: copying, answering phones, making tea, etc. [See essay on page 67.]

One-Cup Sake: Small servings of *sake* (fermented rice wine) available from vending machines and generally purchased by blue-collar types. The *sake* comes from the machine in a glass or plastic cup and can be heated, but is usually cold.

Pachinko: A kind of pinball, tilted vertically so that it can be played while seated. Players buy a supply of little steel balls and send them through the machine; those falling into a scoring slot result in a payoff of more balls. Skilled *pachinko* players can end up with buckets of extra balls, which are then exchanged for prizes (usually candy, cigarettes, or household products like detergent) or cash (which is illegal but not uncommon).

Pokka: The name of a popular line of canned coffee drinks available chilled or heated in vending machines throughout Japan. The name of the character Icepocca in *Director Hira Namijirō* [chapter 4] is a combination of this product name and the name of Chrysler chairman Lee Iacocca.

Salaryman: One of the millions of ordinary salaried businessmen who are the driving force of Japan's companies. Traditionally, salarymen are hired by their company right out of college, and move through the ranks in a fairly predictable manner until retirement.

Yakitori: Chunks of boneless chicken meat and various chicken body parts, seasoned, skewered, and grilled over an open fire. Since *yakitori* is popular as a snack while or after drinking, tiny *yakitori* restaurants are often found in the entertainment districts, usually with a big red lantern out front to attract attention.

When we originally conceived this project, in the spring of 1994, our idea was simply to compile into book form all of the business-related manga (comics) that had previously appeared in *Mangajin*, our magazine of Japanese language learning and pop culture. At that time, we planned to present the manga in the same format they appear in the magazine, i.e., with the Japanese text in the balloons and detailed translations (what we call "four-line format": the original Japanese; readings of the Japanese in English letters; a literal, word-for-word translation; and a final, smooth translation) on the facing pages. It was to be a very simple project—a compilation, really, of work we had already completed.

Obviously, the book we eventually produced is a far cry from our original concept. This is largely because the more we thought about it, the more we realized that it should be read by as many people as possible. Our magazine is an effective vehicle for communicating contemporary Japanese society to non-Japanese, but because of its strong emphasis on language learning, it appeals to a rather limited readership. It is sometimes frustrating to us that the cultural insights *Mangajin* offers do not reach a wider audience—all those who have an interest in Japan, who do business with Japan, who read about Japan in the newspapers and wonder what's true and what isn't, but who lack the time or inclination to study the Japanese language. These are the people for whom we created *Bringing Home the Sushi*.

Besides adding some manga that never appeared in the magazine (several selections of *Evolution of the Office Lady*, *Don't Cry, Tanaka-kun!*, and *Salaryman Seminar*, as well as some pages of *I'm #1!* and *Director Hira Namijirō*), the main departure we made from our original plan was to put English directly in the balloons. This presented its own set of challenges, two of which merit some discussion.

First, it required that we cope somehow with the fact that English and Japanese are read in different directions. The ideal solution would have been to flip the manga pages so that they move left-to-right, as English does. But the creativity of Japanese manga artists—who draw frames in different shapes and sizes, frequently spread text (particularly sound effects) across more than one frame, and occasionally run frames top-to-bottom on an otherwise right-to-left-reading page—effectively ruled out this approach. The only other option (short of redesigning the pages, which would surely have destroyed the feeling of the original works) is the one we chose: leaving the manga in their original form and numbering the balloons in the order they are to be read. While this is not an ideal solution, since it basically asks the reader to read each page backwards, we do believe it offers the best compromise, allowing the English reader to appreciate the artistry of the original manga while simultaneously reading the story in his or her native tongue.

The second challenge presented by the English-in-the-balloons format involved translation. For many reasons, not the least of which is radically different grammatical structures, Japanese and English do not translate easily into one another. The four-line-format we use in the magazine evolved as a solution to that very problem, allowing us to give both a very literal translation and a smooth-sounding final translation. Putting English in the balloons, however, narrowed us down to one translation. In other words, we often had to choose between rendering the original Japanese faithfully and presenting the final English readably.

As will soon be obvious to those of our readers who can compare our translations with the original Japanese along the bottom of the pages, we leaned heavily on the side of readable English. Some translators may disagree with our approach, but we wanted the manga in English to be as natural and fun to read as they are in Japanese, and the only way to achieve that goal was to take liberties with the text. Those who have some familiarity with Japanese and who want to know how things were phrased in the original can refer to the Japanese at the bottom. Indeed, it was in part to satisfy such readers that we included the original Japanese. Our other reason was to enable both native Japanese and native English speakers to use the text as a language-learning aid. For the native English speakers, we took the additional step of adding *furigana*.

As mentioned above, we designed the book the way we did in order to reach as wide an audience as possible. We did this because we believe that among the profusion of books in English that attempt to shed light on Japanese society, Japanese business, or the Japanese people, *Bringing Home the Sushi* stands alone. Too many books profess to explain the "real" Japan. In the belief that the "real" anything can only ever come through authentic, original source materials, we present these nine manga selections. They are the Japanese as the Japanese see themselves; they are the thoughts, the fears, the hopes, and the disappointments of everyday people going through their everyday lives in the complex fabric of the Japanese workplace.

Our concession to exposition is the introductory essays. Because these manga were written by Japanese for Japanese consumption, a great deal of background knowledge is assumed on the part of the reader. The Japanese who read these manga know about the lives of salarymen, housewives, and Office Ladies; indeed, most of them *are* salarymen, housewives, and Office Ladies. We included the introductory essays by Japan experts to allow our American readers to catch up. The manga are enjoyable on their own, but to understand the significance of the events that occur in the stories, and to what extent the stories reflect or depart from reality, it is essential to read the essays.

We almost subtitled this book "The Human Side of Japanese Business," because that is above all what we are trying to communicate. Close relations notwithstanding, a great deal of stereotyping remains on the part of both Americans and Japanese in their perceptions of one another. This is particularly true of perceptions of Japanese salarymen, so often portrayed in the American media as antlike automatons. If nothing else, we would like to think that those who read this book will begin to understand how very human Japanese salarymen are.

Laura K. Silverman
September 27, 1995

Bringing Home the Sushi

An Inside Look at Japanese Business through Japanese Comics

Introduction

Japanese Manga and Japanese Business Culture
by Tomofusa Kure
translated by Elizabeth Baldwin

The Manga Phenomenon—Only in Japan

Foreigners in Japan are always amazed by the profusion of manga. Walk into any bookstore or pass by any train station kiosk and they are front and center; step onto a train and passengers young and old are poring over them. They are as popular among college students and businesspeople as they are among teenagers.

Foreigners are also surprised—and generally displeased—to discover how many of these comics depict scenes of sex and violence. Indeed, it is not unusual for foreigners to fire off letters to the editors of Japanese newspapers to convey their disapproval.

But to my mind, such criticism reveals a lack of understanding of cultural differences. Japanese people have become quite accustomed to, and accepting of, Euro-American culture over the last century; for example, they have lost much of their discomfort at the sight of a man and woman making out lustfully in public, a custom that was considered to be quite lewd until very recently. Meanwhile, nursing in public, which used to carry no sense of shame, has all but disappeared in Japan. Until 30 years ago Japanese women never hesitated to expose their breasts in a bus or train car in order to nurse.

These days, as all aspects of life increasingly conform to Euro-American values, manga alone continue to gain in popularity as a quintessentially Japanese medium. Consequently, foreigners following trends in Japanese intellectual development focus on manga as a critical element of present-day Japanese culture.

The following numbers illustrate the extent to which manga dominate Japanese culture. According to statistics compiled in 1994, annual sales of all publications amount to ¥2.5 trillion. Of this, ¥350 billion are comprised of manga magazines and ¥250 billion of manga books. In other words, sales of manga magazines and books account for one-fourth of the total of the publishing market. Of magazines (weeklies, bi-weeklies, and monthlies) with print runs of over one million, twelve, topped by *Shōnen Jump*, are manga magazines; only one general magazine, *Ie no Hikari*, an educational and entertainment publication published and distributed by the Federation of Agricultural Cooperative Associations, can make this claim.

But sheer numbers do not tell the whole story regarding the success of manga. Manga are thriving in terms of quality as well, as indicated by the continual production of works of extremely high caliber. Indeed, newspapers have reported cases of plagiarized manga making their way into literature. Clearly, manga have become a form of expression embracing everything from pulp for the masses to refined intellectual works. In this way they are no different from conventional fiction, which includes philosophical novels, romances, mysteries, and rank pornography.

Non-Japanese appear to have difficulty comprehending this phenomenon. Generally speaking, so do Japanese born before the war. But the baby boomers, born just after the war, grew up in the middle of the post-war manga culture. As they became college students in the late 1960s, manga evolved into an edifying medium with an appeal for adults in order to hold their interest. The range of themes and expressive techniques expanded.

This group never did put their manga books away, and they and those who followed came to be called the "manga generation." Now pushing 50, they are a core presence in nearly every societal group, and their influence on general attitudes toward manga is palpable.

Manga and the Business World

Businessmen, the core of the Japanese economy, didn't begin to read manga in great numbers until recently, i.e., until after 1970.

Through the 1960s the comics businessmen read were limited to single-frame political cartoons and humorous four-framers that featured appealing main characters, both of which were run in newspapers and general weeklies. Such manga still appear in newspapers and weeklies but, squeezed hard by the invasion of manga magazines (which until the 1960s targeted young boys and girls, and occasionally teenagers, but never adults), they lack their early glory.

With the beginning of the 1970s the previously mentioned "manga generation" entered adulthood. They started college still clutching their manga, and when they moved on to the work force, they did not graduate from manga. The generation that experienced the student revolts of the 1960s was primed to rebel against prevailing cultural values. The disdain of their elders for manga did not impress them. They read the new comics for adults, and they read kids' comics too.

The nature of Japanese fiction also had a bearing on this phenomenon. Modern Japanese literature, which originated during the Meiji Period, tended to eschew the telling of a story, developing instead into a medium which probed the depths of the human psyche. As a result, by the 1970s it had lost vitality, and readers— including intellectuals—had lost interest. Meanwhile, manga offered a new form of expression, as they fashioned even basic human emotions into dramatic stories. Thus they gained the notice of young intellectuals, whose attraction to the new form must have resembled the thrill experienced by Western artists in the first half of the century upon encountering the simple but powerful arts of Asia and Africa.

As the 1980s began, manga were becoming increasingly expressive. Both entertainment and intellectual manga developed considerably. The older members of the manga generation, now in their mid-thirties, filled the middle ranks of businesses. Many, of course, gravitated to different kinds of reading, to sports, or to other leisure pursuits; but generally speaking, the anticipated contempt for manga failed to materialize.

In the fall of 1986 Shōtaro Ishinomori's *Japan Inc.* was published. Its hard cover and high price presented the book as a clear departure from past comics, and yet it became a bestseller in Japan and widely read abroad as well. Sequels and imitations followed.

From the standpoint of expressive technique, *Japan Inc.* was not significant; explanatory diagrams had already been utilized in children's educational manga for half a century, and this technique was simply adopted by Ishinomori to explain economic principles to adults. Rather, it was from the standpoint of influence on the manga world that *Japan Inc.* earned its place. First, "informative manga" (also called "explanatory manga") became a major genre providing needed income to a group of aging artists. Second, businessmen now had an excuse to buy manga: they needed it "for work." (In fact, the new genre even diminished the manga resistance of the older generation.) Third, manga came to be used extensively in education, publicity, promotion, and other areas. Thus, while the advent of "informative manga" did not contribute to the development of manga as a form, it had an enormous impact on the manga industry, affecting creators, publishers, and related industries in the tertiary sector.

The Portrayal of Businessmen in Manga until the 1980s

Reading manga is a normal activity for Japanese businessmen, and many comics feature businessmen as main characters. Not surprisingly, the manner in which they are depicted has varied with the times, reflecting real-life changes in businessmen, the subset of salarymen, and the society of which they are a part.

Until the 1960s the word "salaryman" connoted a rather drab occupation and low socioeconomic status. It was the sons of the unpropertied class who labored as salarymen, receiving salaries that were determined by their companies and being granted little opportunity to exercise their abilities. Throughout the 1960s a mere 10 to 20 percent of these men had attended four- or two-year colleges; most were high school or even junior high school graduates. As this population figured increasingly in hit songs and popular fiction, the "pitiful salaryman" became a household term.

During the 1970s Japan's economic structure underwent a transformation, impelling gradual change in both the occupation and the socioeconomic level of the salaryman. As most economic activity shifted to corporations, the numbers of farmers, fishermen, craftsmen, and small business proprietors steadily dwindled, while the occupation of "salaryman" absorbed more and more members. Meanwhile, the educational level of the Japanese continued to climb. In the early 1970s those advancing to college or junior college surpassed 20 percent. By the middle of the decade this number hovered around 35 percent. Some companies began to base salary on ability as well as seniority, and in time a respectable number of salarymen became pillars of large corporations. In other words, they became "businessmen."

Manga, of course, reflected these changes. The "pitiful salaryman" of the 1970s was joined in the 1980s by the "elite businessman." Before discussing this transition, however, it seems appropriate to give a brief overview of manga during the 1970s.

As mentioned above, until the late 1960s the manga read by adults were extremely brief, consisting for the most part of single-frame and four-frame comics run in newspapers and general weeklies. Main characters were usually "ordinary guys" with whom the reader could easily identify; many were "pitiful salarymen." In general, the comics conformed to set patterns: failures at work, nonsensical jokes exchanged with co-workers, amusing family anecdotes, and the like. The market for such manga, which reflect a timeless sort of humor, remains strong, and so they continue to be generated.

But the situation changed greatly in the late 1960s with the arrival of Sadao Shōji. Using an unprecedented wavy style of drawing that appeared rather crude at first glance, he smashed the stereotypical image of the "pitiful salaryman." The "pitiful" quality Shōji created came from his attention to detail and portrayal of concrete situations. In one typical story, the main character falsifies a commuter ticket coupon in order to get one thousand yen. This allows him first to add a ¥300 order of fries to his meal. He then plays *pachinko* with the remaining ¥700 and in his fervor manages to lose ¥1,500, ending up with a net loss of ¥500.

Through his uniquely rough and unpretentious renderings, Shōji managed to depict this and other stereotype-shattering scenes of real life. His manga are currently gaining renewed attention amid growing recognition that it was precisely his genius with the ordinary that made his comics so easy to overlook in the beginning. In fact, Shōji's work marked the beginning of the genre of salaryman manga. To this day, he along with his many followers continue to keep the genre fresh.

The mid-1970s saw the appearance of the work of a brilliant gag manga artist named Tatsuhiko Yamagami. Employing an intense black humor, he redefined the Japanese concept of what is funny. Yamagami's humor was too radical to depict salarymen; his contribution lay in raising the techniques for eliciting mirth to a new level.

At the same time, Masatoshi Furuya was gaining popularity with his *unchiku* ("knowledge-intensive") *manga*. He depicted a father who, though a loser at the office, manifested his talents at home through cooking and Sunday carpentry. This father gained his family's confidence by demonstrating his endless store of knowledge on the subject of food and furniture. The success of this manga helped prepare the way for *Diary of a Fishing Freak*, which began in 1979, and the informative manga that came after 1986.

The Portrayal of Businessmen in Manga since the 1980s

The 1980s brought variety to the images of salarymen and businessmen being portrayed in manga. As more and more people entered the profession, the single stereotype of the "pitiful salaryman" became woefully inadequate. Of course, the low-brow comics that capitalized on this stereotype maintained their popularity, as they continued to appeal to readers who related to and were comforted by the image.

The first new type of business manga featured salarymen who were concerned less with job and promotions than with hobbies or family. The prime example is *Diary of a Fishing Freak*, the main character of which is a fishing nut who is rather indifferent to his job. His good nature, however, endears him to his co-workers, and through fishing he even befriends members of his industry's inner circle. The ever-increasing adherents to the "my home" principle, a major tenet of "me-ism," are devoted to this series.

The second new genre depicted the elite core of businessmen. Started in 1983, *Section Chief Kōsaku Shima*, by Kenshi Hirokane, launched this genre. In *Kōsaku Shima*, Hirokane created an eminently lifelike character: a graduate of a famous university and employee of a major corporation, intelligent, sensible, full of energy, and caught up in a continuous swirl of love affairs. Of course, real businessmen are rarely as glamorous as Shima, but the situations in which he was placed were consistently realistic, and the series was always fresh. The success of *Kōsaku Shima* speaks to the ability of hundreds of thousands of readers to relate in some way to Shima's lifestyle. It must also be noted that this was the era of manga, and businessmen were among manga's greatest fans. The previously mentioned *Japan Inc.* appeared three years after this series began.

The popularity of *Section Chief Kōsaku Shima* spawned business manga of every type, from those depicting entry-level salarymen making their way to the fast track to those featuring elite businesswomen. There were even those, like *Way of an Osaka Loan Shark* by Yūji Aoki, that ventured into the underworld of the Japanese mafia.

Japan is currently mired in a recession brought about by the bursting of the bubble economy and the rising yen. The birth rate is falling and the population aging. As these changes occur, we can predict that the new realities will generate new manga images of salarymen and businessmen.

日本の漫画と日本のビジネス社会

呉　智英

1.　世界に類を見ない日本マンガ

　日本に来た外国人が一様に驚くのがマンガがあふれていることである。町の書店でも駅の売店でもさまざまなマンガ雑誌が売られ、電車の中で大人たちがそれを読んでいる。大学でも会社でもマンガは広く読まれている。しかも、そこには性的な話や暴力的な物語もしばしば描かれている。こうした光景を見た外国人が日本の新聞にこれを批判する投書をすることもよくある。

　しかし、こういう批判や違和感は文化の差を理解できていないからである。欧米の文化にこの一世紀でずいぶん慣れ、寛容になった日本人は、西洋人の男女が人前で口を吸い合うことを奇異に思わなくなったが、ついこの間まではこれを猥褻な習慣だと思っていた。一方で、三十年程前まで、日本女性は電車やバスの中で乳房を出して赤ん坊に授乳することに平気だった。人前での授乳に羞恥の感情は起きなかったのである。もっとも、今では全ての生活が欧米化される中で、この生活習慣もなくなってしまった。しかし、マンガだけは、きわめて日本的な文化メディアとして、ますます隆盛であり、日本文化史に関心のある外国人は重要な現代日本文化の一つとしてこれに注目している。

　マンガがどれほど隆盛であるかは、最近の統計から次の数字を見てもらえばわかるだろう。統計によると、1994年の全出版物の年間売上げは二兆五千億円にのぼるが、このうちマンガ雑誌が三千五百億円、またマンガ単行本は二千五百億円を占めている。つまり、マンガ雑誌とマンガ単行本の年間売上げ合計が、全出版物の年間売上げの四分の一を占めている。発行部数百万部を超える雑誌（週刊、隔週刊、月刊）には「少年ジャンプ」以下、十二のマンガ誌が含まれるが、一般誌では、農協が組織的に販売する教養・誤楽誌である「家の光」一誌だけである。

　マンガの隆盛は量的な面だけではない。質的な面においても、きわめて高度な作品が生み出され、マンガから文学への盗作が新聞の話題になることがある。このように、マンガは、高尚で知的な作品から大衆的な作品まで広く含む表現様式にまで成長している。それは、文学という表現様式が、哲学的な小説も、社会的テーマを扱ったルポルタージュも、通俗的な恋愛小説や探偵小説も、低俗なポルノグラフィも、すべて含んでいるのと同じことである。

　ただ、このことは外国人には理解されにくい。日本人でも、おおむね、戦前生まれの人はそうである。戦後ほどなく生まれた人たちは、生まれた時か

8

ら戦後マンガの文化状況の中で育ってきた。彼らが大学生になる頃、すなわ
ち、1960年代後半、この人たちを対象としてマンガは教養ある大人でも読め
るものに変身した。テーマは拡大し、表現技術は進歩した。この人たちは、
以後マンガを手離すことはなかった。この人たち以降の人たちを"マンガ世
代"と呼ぶ。彼らは今、五十歳目前であり、社会の各界で中核的存在であ
る。そのため、マンガについての社会的認知もずいぶん変わってきている。

2. ビジネス社会とマンガ
　日本経済を中心的に支えるビジネスマンがこんなに広くマンガを読むよう
になったのは最近のことである。1970年代に入るまではこんなことはなかっ
た。
　1960年代までは、ビジネスマンが読むマンガは限られていた。新聞や一般
の週刊誌に載っている政治諷刺の一コママンガや親しみやすい主人公をユー
モラスに描いた四コママンガぐらいであった。こういう一コママンガや四コ
ママンガは、もちろん、今も新聞や一般の週刊誌に連載されているが、マン
ガ雑誌の勢に圧されて過去の栄光はなくなっている。1960年代までは、マン
ガ雑誌は少年少女向けのものが中心で、一部に青年向けのものが出始めてい
たが、大人が読むものではなかった。
　しかし、1970年代に入る頃、前述したマンガ世代が大人の仲間入りを始
めた。彼らは大学生になってもマンガを手離さず、社会人になっても、なお
マンガから卒業しなかった。彼らは1960年代後半の"学生叛乱の時代"を体
験していたので、既成の文化的価値に反することをするのに抵抗感を持って
いなかった。旧世代がマンガを読むことを冷たく見ていても意に介さなかっ
た。彼らは大人向けに描かれたマンガも読んだし、少年向けに描かれたマン
ガも読んだ。
　これには、日本文学の特殊事情が関係している。明治に始まる日本近代文
学は、骨格のしっかりしたドラマよりも、人間の内面心理を描くことに力を
入れ、その結果躍動感を失い、1970年代には知的な人々の間でさえ人気をな
くしつつあった。一方、マンガは、興隆する新しい表現形式として、人間の
原初的な感情をもドラマに仕立て、知的な青年たちをも魅了した。それは、
今世紀前半の美術家が、アジア・アフリカの素朴ではあるが力強い美術に興
奮を覚えたのに近いだろう。
　1980年代に入ると、マンガの表現技術はさらに豊かになり、娯楽作品も高
尚なテーマを扱った作品も、ともに大きく発達した。また、マンガ世代は三
十歳代の半ばにまで成長し、ビジネス社会の中堅層になった。もちろん、彼
らの中に、マンガ以外の本やスポーツなどに関心が移る者も大勢いたが、彼
らには総じてマンガへの反感がなかったことが重要である。
　1986年秋、海外でも広く知られている石ノ森章太郎『マンガ・日本経済入
門』が出た。それまで、マンガは軽装版のものが多かったが、これはハード
カバーであり、いくぶん高価だったが、それでもベストセラーになった。続
編や模倣本も出た。
　この本は、二つの観点から論じることができる。
　一つは、マンガ表現の可能性という観点である。この観点から見ると、

『マンガ・日本経済入門』には、何の新味もない。マンガには図解機能があり、これを応用して、子供向けに学習マンガというものが半世紀も前から存在していた。それを経済という大人向けのテーマに応用しただけのことである。発達したマンガの表現技術がそれを可能にしたのであって、この作品が新しい表現の可能性を開発したのではない。事実、作者の石ノ森は既に盛りを過ぎた作家であり、1970年代以降、衝撃力のある作品は描いていなかった。この作品の模倣作や類似作を描いたマンガ家たちも、誰もが盛りを過ぎた作家であり、過去の高い知名度を利用しただけであった。力をなくした映画スターが、かつての名を利用してレストランを始め、それが大成功したからといって、映画に新しい未来が出現するわけではないのと同じである。

　もう一つは、マンガの社会への影響力という観点である。この観点からは、『マンガ・日本経済入門』は重要な作品である。第一に、この作品に代表される“情報マンガ”（入門マンガとも解説マンガとも呼ばれる）が一つの大きなジャンルとなり、盛りを過ぎて収入もなくなった老大家たちに仕事を与えたことである。第二に、ビジネスマンたちに仕事の資料としてマンガを手に取る言い分を与え、旧世代の人たちにもマンガへの違和感を少なくさせた。第三に、教育、広報、宣伝、などの分野に、マンガを取り入れる風潮が広がった。

　以上二つの観点をまとめて言うと、情報マンガの登場は、マンガという表現様式の発達に寄与するものは何もなかったけれど、産業としてのマンガには、作者にとっても出版社にとっても、その他の第三次産業にとっても、大きな意味を持った、ということになる。

3．　ビジネスマンはマンガにどう描かれてきたか——1980年代以前
　日本ではビジネスマンがごく当り前にマンガ雑誌を読んでいる。マンガの内容もビジネスマンを主人公にしたものがかなりある。ただ、そこには時代ごとに世相を反映した変化があった。マンガの変化は、ビジネスマンやそれを含むサラリーマン像の変化、さらには日本社会の変化を表わしている。

　1960年代までの日本では、サラリーマンという職業・階級は地味なものだとされていた。とりたてて資産のない階級の息子たちが就く職業であり、収入は会社の規定によって決められており、手腕を発揮する余地は少ないものだったからである。また、大学・短大への進学率は、1960年代を通じて10%から20%の間であり、サラリーマンの大多数は中学か高校を卒業した学歴の人たちであった。こういう人たちを描いた流行歌や大衆小説に人気があり、そこでは“しがないサラリーマン”という決まり文句が使われた。

　1970年代に入ってから、サラリーマンという職業・階級は少しずつ変わりだす。日本の経済構造が大きく変化し、農家、漁師、職人、小規模自営業、といった職業が少なくなり、経済活動のほとんどを企業が占めるようになった。必然的にサラリーマンという職業の人が多くなった。国民の学歴も上がり、大学・短大の進学率は、1970年代初めに20%を超え、1970年代の半ば以降は35%前後に達するようになった。給与も、年功序列の他に能力を重視する会社が現われた。こうして、大企業の柱となるサラリーマン、すなわち「ビジネスマン」と呼ばれる人たちが相当数登場することになる。

マンガもこうした社会の変化を反映している。マンガに描かれたサラリーマン像は、1970年代までは、“しがないサラリーマン”が多く、1980年代に入って、“エリートのビジネスマン”が登場するようになる。そこで、これを区切ってその時代とマンガを見てみることにする。

　まず、1970年代までである。

　先に述べたように、1960年代の後半までは、大人の読むマンガは新聞や一般雑誌に連載されるごく短い作品（多くは一コマか四コマ作品）でしかなかった。こうした作品には、親しみ深い庶民を主人公にしたものが多く、“しがないサラリーマン”もしばしば描かれた。しかし、それらはきわめて類型的なものであった。会社での失敗、同僚と交すたわいないジョーク、家庭での微笑ましい逸話、こうしたどんな時代にもある笑いが描かれた。そして、こうしたマンガへの需要は、当然ながら現在も根強くあり、今もこのジャンルは生きのびている。

　しかし、1960年代の後半に、東海林さだおが登場して、事情は大きく変わる。彼は、それまでのマンガになかった一見弱々しく粗雑に見える描線で、類型的な“しがないサラリーマン像”を打ち砕いた。彼の描くしがなさは、細部にこだわり、具体的だった。交通費の伝票を改竄して千円浮かし、それで昼食に三百円のフライを一品余計に食べ、残りの七百円でパチンコをやり、熱くなって千五百円すって、結局、五百円のむだづかい、というように、類型化されない日常生活を、リアルに、しかしリアルではない描線で自嘲的に描いた。彼の天才ぶりは、あまりにも当り前すぎて誰もが見逃していたことに再度注目するという着眼に現われている。東海林さだおの登場によって、サラリーマンガという新しいジャンルが成立し、後続者が輩出した。東海林は今なお健筆をふるっている。

　1970年代半ば、山上たつひこという天才的なギャグマンガ家が登場した。彼は強烈なブラックユーモアで笑いの範囲を広げた。その笑いは過激であり、サラリーマンを描くには適していなかった。しかし、笑いの技術は彼の登場によって格段に進歩した。

　同じ頃、古谷三敏が“うんちくマンガ”で人気を集めた。会社では必ずしも有能ではないが、家に帰ると、料理や日曜大工といった趣味の領域で才能を発揮し、また食材や家具などについてうんちくを披瀝し、そのことによって家族の信頼を得る父親をユーモラスに描いた。この作品の成功が、1979年から始まった『釣りバカ日誌』（やまさき十三作、北見けんいち画）や1986年以後の情報マンガの出現を準備したと見ることができる。

４．ビジネスマンはマンガにどう描かれてきたか─1980年代以降

　1980年代に入って、マンガに描かれるサラリーマン・ビジネスマン像は多様化した。サラリーマンを職業とする人が飛躍的にふえることによって、単一の“しがないサラリーマン”という類型では、それを描けなくなったからである。むろん、“しがないサラリーマン”を描いた凡庸なマンガは、それが凡庸であるだけに、根強い人気はある。

　新しく登場したのは、第一に、出世や仕事より趣味や家族愛に生きるサラリーマンを描いたマンガである。典型は前述の『釣りバカ日誌』である。主

人公はあまり仕事に熱心でない釣りマニアのサラリーマンだが、人柄の良さによって同僚からも愛され、釣りを通じて実業界の中枢の人たちとも友人となる。ミーイズムの典型であるマイホーム主義が社会に広まったが、そういう人たちに愛読されている。

　第二が、エリートビジネスマンを描いたマンガである。1983年に始まった『課長・島耕作』（弘兼憲史）がその開発者である。有名大学卒、大企業の社員、衰えを知らぬ容貌、知性と良識、何人もの女性との恋愛…という現実味のあるヒーローが作られた。もちろん、実際のビジネスマンがこの主人公のようにかっこいいわけはないのだが、舞台設定に現実味を感じさせるところに新味があった。いうまでもなく、この主人公に感情移入できるビジネスマンたちが何十万人も読者として潜在している時代になったから、この作品は成功したのである。また、産業の主力部隊であるビジネスマンがマンガに反感を抱かないマンガ世代になっていたからでもある。初めの方で述べた『マンガ・日本経済入門』の登場は『課長・島耕作』開始の三年後のことである。

　この作品の人気によって、エリートの卵である新人ビジネスマンを描いた作品や女性のエリートビジネスマンを主人公にしたマンガも現われた。

　こうした一方で、1990年には、社会の暗部、人間の暗部を描いた『ナニワ金融道』（青木雄二）のような異色のビジネスマンガも登場した。作者の青木は当時既に四十五歳になる新人であった。絵は一見稚拙ながら不思議なユーモアが感じられた。街の高利の金融屋にふとしたことから勤めるようになった主人公の青年が見た暗いドラマが、この絵の力によってすくいを感じさせている。

　現在、日本のビジネス社会は、バブル経済崩壊と円高とによる不況の中にある。また、少子社会、高齢化社会にもなりつつある。こうした中で、新たなビジネスマン・サラリーマン像を描くマンガが出てくることに期待したい。

Human Crossroads

Author: Masao Yajima   Artist: Kenshi Hirokane

Essay by Peter Duus

The Japanese used to say that four things were to be feared in life: earthquakes, lightning, fires, and the "old man." In those days, the father reigned supreme. The law made him the sole custodian of the family property, and society expected him to be its chief disciplinarian. It was also the father's job to educate his sons in his craft or occupation, whether it was farming, carpentry, or shopkeeping.

As the manga series *Human Crossroads* makes clear, the father's lot is not what it used to be. The protagonist, Yasuhiro, neither respects nor fears his father. Indeed, at the beginning of the story he cannot even manage to say "Hello" as he passes by his father puttering in the garden. While this might seem strange to Americans who have heard so much about the strength of family ties in Japan, emotional distance between father and son is not at all unusual.

The "economic miracle" of the 1950s and 1960s brought about this change. Rapid industrialization pulled men off the farm and out of the shop. The average father was no longer an independent farmer or small business proprietor but a company employee or "salaryman," whose company drove him hard. The "company warrior" was expected to give his all, including evenings, Saturdays, and sometimes even Sundays too. He worked far longer hours than his counterparts in the United States and Europe—and probably still does, even though he now has weekends off.

The generation to which Yasuhiro's father belonged experienced the uncertainties of the depression, the privations of war, and post-defeat economic hardship. For them the rewards of workaholism were worth it: job security, steadily rising wages, and the promise of promotion. But it was not long before they discovered that there was a downside to long hours as well.

By the late 1960s the "absent father," who left early in the morning and returned late at night, was becoming a stranger to his children. A joke at the time went that instead of saying "See you later" (*Itte irasshai*) when their father left in the morning, more and more young children were saying "Please come again" (*Mata kite, ne*). With the father so rarely at home, his role as an authority figure declined. It was Mama who took responsibility for bringing up and educating the children, while the "old man" handed her his pay envelope and spent Sunday snoozing off his work fatigue. The white-collar father was less fearsome to his children than his own father had been—and more distant from them as well.

The "corporate warrior" was also worn down by the stress and strain of office politics. As in American companies, promotions often depended on buttering up the

13

boss as much as job performance, but in a Japanese firm, office politicking was essential just to keep human relations on an even keel within the workplace. Work did not end when the office day was over. It often continued into the night, as co-workers and their superiors retreated together to bars or cabarets to vent spleen, soothe wounded nerves, or mend relationships damaged during the day.

Even a salaryman with few high hopes or prospects had to cultivate his superiors simply to maintain "harmony" in the office. As we see in the story, Yasuhiro's father is bitter at having to curry favor with his boss, a younger man promoted over him merely because of a college degree. After drinking away more of his pay envelope than he should, he stages the fake mugging his son witnesses.

Yasuhiro, who probably graduated from a good university after his mother shepherded him through cram schools and "examination hell," has done a lot better than his father. Even though his daily commute is longer, his family lives in a comfortable high-rise apartment house in the suburbs, smaller but more convenient and prestigious than his parents' shabby house in a semi-industrial downtown neighborhood. At his own company he seems to have risen higher than his father did.

But Yasuhiro fears he is simply repeating his father's life of quiet desperation, trying to do his best but never quite appreciated by anyone, perhaps not even his wife. His own efforts at office politics buy him the contempt of his subordinates, and he feels the same sense of defeat his father did.

To be sure, Yasuhiro's self-doubts spring from purely personal anxieties: a fear that his own character is as timid, unheroic, gloomy, nitpicking, and whiny as his father's. But in his own way, Yasuhiro may be typical of the current generation of "thirty-something" salarymen, who grew up in a time of increasing affluence wrought by their fathers' generation.

In the 1980s the media tagged this generation as a "new breed" (shinjinrui) of Japanese, unwilling to work as hard as their parents did but expecting to lead a better life. Behind the label lay concern that this generation was losing the work ethic—the workaholism of the "corporate warrior"—needed to keep the economy growing. In fact, what may be most significant about the "new breed" is not any lack of work ethic, but a new sense of priorities. As opportunities for upward advancement have narrowed, this generation has concluded that there may be more to life than the annual bonus or the regular promotion.

Yasuhiro overcomes the distance between himself and his father when he reaches a similar conclusion. As his tipsy elderly father tells him: no matter how well you do at the office everyone ends up at the same finish line. (As John Maynard Keynes once said, "In the long run, we are all dead.") What may be most important in life is the quiet affection he enjoys with his father as they watch the sunset in the late spring sky.

This sentimental ending must be heartening to salaryman readers who share Yasuhiro's feelings. But perhaps the story delivers a barbed message, too. As we contemplate the puzzled look on Yasuhiro's son in the last panel, we wonder: is the emotional gap between father and son here to stay?

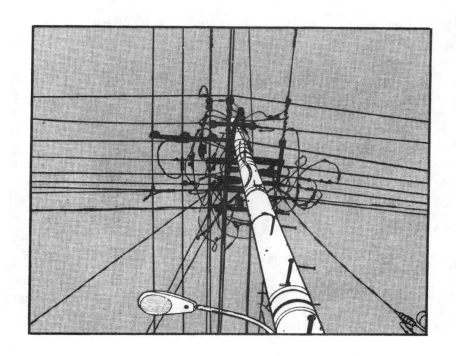

The Telephone Pole

でんちゅう
電柱

I often remember this scene from twenty-five years ago. ①

Hiroshi Haneda ③

Hic! ②

Hic! ⑥

Burp ⑤

Urp! ④

① 私はいつも、二十五年前のこの光景を思い出す。　② ヒクッ　③ 羽田弘　④ ウィッ　⑤ ゲプ　⑥ ヒクッ

① 給料袋　② あ、俺、こんなに遣っちゃったかなあ。　③ ヒクッ

①よし。　②ただいまあ〜ッ　③お、俺さ、今そこで強盗にあっちゃったんだ。　④どうしようもない男だった…　⑤まいったよ　⑥なはははははは　⑦…それが私の父だった。

every time I look at my father's back like this, I think about that time. ②

And now... ①

① そして、今こうやって… ② 父の背中を見るたびにあの時のことを思い出すのだ…

① 康弘ちゃん、久しぶりねえ、立派になって。　②うん？　③…康弘？どこに…　④え？　⑤あれ、今、あんたんとこへ寄ってたんじゃないの？　⑥やだよ。

① 俺は世の中で怖いものなんか何もねえ!! ② キャーッ　やめてえッ ③ うるせえ ④ 悪党なら、まだ恨みようもある。善良なら、愛しようがある。

And if he didn't resemble me, I could forgive him. ①

Sit down a minute. I hate having to say something like this to you, but... ③

Chief, what is it you wanted to see me about? ②

I see... ⑤

watching you recently, I'm a little concerned. But it's not only me. I've been told by the section chief, too, that I should caution you. ④

① そして自分に似ていなければ許しようもある。 ②主任、用事って何ですか？ ③まあ、座れよ、ボクもこんなことを君には言いたくないんだけど… ④最近の君を見てるとどうも不安でねえ、いや、私だけじゃなく課長からも注意するように言われているんだ。 ⑤はあ…

23

① あの主任の言うこと、いちいちセコイの。　② それも全部自分じゃなく、「誰がこう言っている」「誰があ
あ言っている」だぜ、気が小せえくせに立場上文句言ってるわけよ、臆病者が。　③ 文句言ってるテメエのほ
うが、目をキョロキョロさせて情けないったらねえよ。

① 俺はさ、若い奴のためを思ってんだよな。 ②後で困るのはあいつらなわけでさ、上だって俺と同じように評価してると思うんだ。 ③でも、その若い社員の言ってること、あたってるんじゃない。 ④だいたいあなたセコイし、暗すぎるわよ。

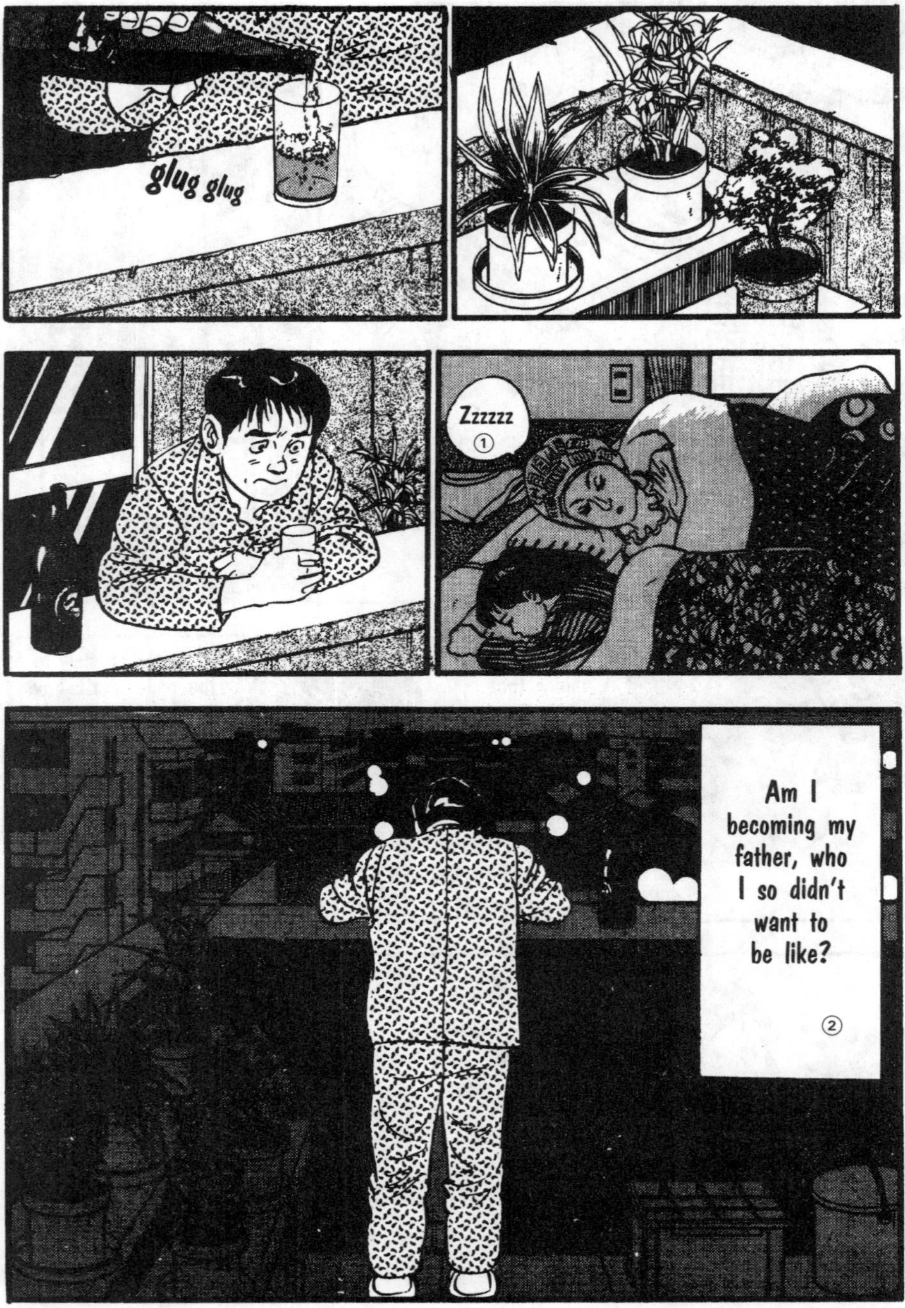

① スースー　② 俺(おれ)は、あんなになりたくないと思(おも)っていた父(ちち)に似(に)てきたのだろうか…

① ど　どうぞ課長!!　② 居酒屋きらく　③ いや、今日は本当にごくろうさまでした。課長がいなかったらど
うなっていたか、それを考えると今でも冷や汗が出ますよ。　④ なはははははは！　⑤ 居酒屋きらく
⑥ 父の勤める工場のそばに住んでいたせいもあって、私はよく父を目にしたものだった…

① 冗談じゃないよ。バカヤロー!! ② おでん ③ ちょっとおだてりゃ、その気になりやがって、課長、課長ってあいつ俺より年下なんだぜ!! ④ ウィッヒック ⑤ 大学出たってだけで俺の上に来やがってよ!! ⑥ うるせえな! 静かに飲むか、帰るか、どっちかにしろい!! ⑦ あ…すみません。 ⑧ あの…領収書もらえますか。 ⑨ 電柱の陰で見る父はいつも卑屈で、臆病で、ズルくてセコく酔っていた。

① 今_{いま}の私_{わたし}のように… ② 何_{なに}してるのあなた…そんなところで。　③うん。　④もう寝_ねたら、明日_{あした}また大変_{たいへん}よ。
⑤うん。

For better or for worse, I can't live near work. At least there's no danger of my children watching me from behind telephone poles...

①

① 幸か不幸か、今の私は子供達にその姿を見られるほどそばに勤めていない。そばに住めないから電柱の陰で見られる心配もないが…

① …おやじ。 ②生

① もうすぐ夏だなあ… ② ああ。 ③ 何かあったのか？ ④ どうして？ ⑤ めずらしいからさ、家に寄るなんて　母さんの命日でもないし、用事があったんだろう。 ⑥ ないよ…何も。 ⑦ おやじ、俺に自分がどんな人間に思われてると思う？ ⑧ さあな、どう思うってほどの男じゃないし、おまえが知ってるだけの人間だ。そして今はただのジジイだ。

Yeah, there's nothing you can do about it, I guess. ②

I suppose that's what I'll become as well. ①

Wealthy people and poor people and important people and not-so-important people—they're all the same when they've passed on. ④

People's lives are all pretty much alike. Even if you think you've accomplished all kinds of things, in the end it never amounts to much. ③

Whether because of his age, or because he hadn't had anyone to talk to since my mother's death, or perhaps because he was drinking for the first time in a long time, my father was unusually talkative. ⑤

I was suddenly overcome by the temptation to ask him about that night— ⑥

①俺もそうなるんだろうか？　②ああ、しょうがないだろ。　③人間の人生なんてみんな似たりよったりさ、いろんなことをやって来たように思っても、しょせん大したことはないのさ。　④金持ちも貧乏人も偉い奴も偉くない奴もみんな過ぎ去ってしまえば同じだ。　⑤年のせいなのか、母が死んで話し相手がいなくなったせいなのか、あるいは久しぶりに飲む酒のせいか、父はいつになく多弁だった。　⑥俺は突然、あの夜のことを聞いてみたい誘惑にかられた…

—about the fake mugging he had staged to cover up spending his paycheck, never even knowing that I was watching. ①

No, I don't know what you're talk-ing about. ③

Huh? ②

I regretted having asked. Even if I was drunk, what sense was there in mak-ing an old man remember a shameful event from the distant past? ⑤

I have no recollection of doing such a thing. You must have mistaken someone else for me. ④

① 私が見ているとも知らずに遣い過ぎた給料をごまかすために演じた狂言強盗のことを… ② うん… ③ いや、知らん。 ④ 俺はそんなことをした覚えはない。おまえ、誰か他の人間と見間違えてるんじゃないのか？ ⑤ 私は後悔した。酔っていたとはいえ、老人に遠い過去の恥を思い出させて何の意味があるというのだ。

The man who was neither a villain nor a man of integrity, who was obsequious and cowardly, and a shifty, whiny drunk——probably just the kind of man I've now become. ③

O D E N ②

He had forgotten what kind of man he had been— the kind of man that I vowed absolutely not to become. ①

Huh? ⑤

Oh! ④

What is it? ⑦

I didn't realize. ⑥

①私が絶対になるまいと心に誓った大人の姿を… ②おでん ③悪党でもなく、善良でもなく、卑屈で、臆病で、ズルくてセコく酔っていた…たぶん今の自分にそっくりな大人の姿を。 ④あ ⑤え？ ⑥気づかなかった… ⑦何ですか？

The image of my father that I recall is an image of him at just about my age right now. Perhaps I was actually trying to see myself by scrutinizing the image of my father...
③

①あ、いや、すみません、お勘定して!! ②あ、それと領収書ちょうだい。 ③私が思い出す父の姿は、ちょうど今の自分の年齢ぐらいの父の姿だ…もしかしたら私は父の姿を借りて自分の姿を追ってるんじゃ… ④はあ ⑤はあ ⑥はあ ⑦はあ ⑧はあ

What's wrong?! ④

Pant ①

Pant ②

Pant ③

Oh? ⑥

Uh, urr...There's something I forgot to say. They're not as nice as these, but I have some plants on the balcony at my place, too. If you'd like, why don't you come and see them from time to time? ⑤

① はあ ② はあ ③ はあ ④ …どうした!? ⑤ あ、ああ…言い忘れてたことがあったんだ…これほど立派じゃないけど、俺の家のベランダにも植木があるんだ。よかったら、たまには見においでよ。 ⑥ そうか…

① おやじ、このまえおもしろいこと言ってたね。人生なんて、みんな似たりよったり、すぎ去ってしまえば同じだって。　②あははは

① もうすぐ夏だな…　② ああ。　③ 何してんだろう…？

Diary of a Fishing Freak

Author: Jūzō Yamasaki   Artist: Ken'ichi Kitami

Essay by Toshimasa Kii and Greg Tenhover

In the beginning of the series *Dairy of a Fishing Freak*, the main character, Hamasaki, is portrayed as a man with a job, a home, and a wife, but no real life to speak of. He shows no ambition in his work at a construction firm, and shies away from the typical Japanese salaryman activities. He doesn't like drinking with his friends because they make him sing karaoke. Golf and mahjongg are too much trouble. He once belonged to a Japanese chess club, but quit playing because he was always beaten by pre-teen players.

On weekends Hamasaki just lies around the house. His wife urges him to find a hobby, largely because she knows socializing through such activities can lead to career advancement. With a child on the way, she is becoming increasingly concerned about their future. Thus, when Hamasaki is invited fishing by his section chief, Sasaki, she is elated.

Sasaki knows fishing, and is his usual arrogant self as he instructs Hamasaki on the finer points. But Hamasaki winds up catching all the fish. He has finally found something he does well, and that he enjoys doing. In no time, he becomes a "fishing freak," and everything else in his life—especially his work—becomes secondary to his new hobby.

Although it is true that the world of the salaryman in Japan is changing, and that the pressure on employees to subordinate their private lives to the interests of the company is easing somewhat, Hamasaki's total lack of interest in advancing his career and his unabashed preference for fishing over work put this character largely in the realm of fantasy. Perhaps even further removed from reality is the attitude of his boss and family, who seem to accept, or at least resign themselves to, his unusual approach to life.

Judging from the phenomenal success of this series in Japan—Shogakukan's 1,000,000+ circulation magazine *Big Comic Original* has featured it since 1979, 37 volumes of the compiled series have been published in book form, and Shochiku, a major movie studio, has made seven movies based on it—this fantasy clearly strikes a responsive chord with many Japanese salarymen who are still under pressure to perform and conform.

The salaryman fantasy played out in this particular episode reaches a peak when not only Hamasaki but also his by-the-book boss Sasaki tell off an extremely important businessman from whom they are trying to solicit a contract. In corporate Japan, where virtually all relationships bear a hierarchical aspect, the relationship between client and supplier is particularly polarized. Moreover, no situation demands quite the degree of kowtowing that entertaining a prospective client does. Despite all of that, Hamasaki and Sasaki let their personal feelings toward this rather pompous and arrogant man override their need to act with the propriety—and obsequiousness—that the situation demands.

Such conduct would be a serious breach of etiquette in almost any society, but to appreciate how shocking it would be in Japan, it helps to know something about the concepts of *tatemae* and *honne*.

Tatemae and *Honne*

In all societies there can be conflict between a person's real desires and the rules of the group. But to the Japanese, who perceive harmonious relationships as the very foundation of a stable society, the dichotomy between what one wants to do and how one is expected to behave takes on particular importance. The Japanese have two words that neatly reflect and define these conflicting interests: *tatemae* and *honne*.

Tatemae is the principles and expectations of the group, the outward appearance, the "public" truth, or, if you will, the "party line." The word *tatemae* is written with two Chinese characters, the first meaning "build" or "raise," and the second, "front" or "before." So *tatemae* is literally the structure or face of the building, the part people see. The word is similar in meaning to the English word "facade," which has the dual meanings of "front" and "artificial" or "false." In relationships, *tatemae* is the face you show others.

Honne, by contrast, is a person's genuine feelings and opinions—what Americans might call the "real" truth. The first character suggests "main," "true," or "real." The second character refers to a "sound," "tone," or "voice." *Honne*, therefore, is the "true sound," something like the idiomatic "true colors" in English. Unless the situation allows, *honne* is generally kept under wraps.

The importance of knowing when it is okay to express *honne* and when it isn't cannot be overstated. Indeed, Hamasaki's rather tenuous grasp of this principle is the primary reason for Sasaki's reluctance to bring him along to such an important meeting. Sasaki, by contrast, is a perfect model of *tatemae* in action, at least until the end of the evening.

While it is a little farfetched that anyone, even a character like Hamasaki, would verbally assault a client, disregard for social conventions on the part of someone as assimilated into Japanese norms of behavior as Sasaki is truly unlikely. It is worth noting, however, that while Hamasaki loses control of his emotions, shouting and posturing, Sasaki tells the client off without raising his voice. He loses his *tatemae*, but not his cool.

The ending, in which the client calls Sasaki, apologizes for his self-centered views, and offers the contract, is certainly hard to imagine, but it is perhaps not totally preposterous to a Japanese reader. We might infer that many Japanese would indeed like to express their *honne* more often, and, in fact, feel a certain respect for those who do.

42

"One Cup" Fisherman ①

Idiot!
It's tangled.
Don't pull!
②

As a result, a pleasant discussion about fishing can suddenly turn into a stormy debate.
④

Veteran fishermen each have their own personal views about fishing.
③

① ワンカップ釣り師　② 馬鹿ッ　マツリだ　引くな!!　③ 釣りのベテランは各々一家言を持っているもの
であります。　④ それが時として、和やかな釣り談義を一変、険悪なムードにしてしまうこともあるので
す。

Fishing fanatic Densuke Hamasaki works at a mid-sized construction company in the center of the city. ①

The commute from his old, government-owned apartment building takes a little over an hour. ②

① 釣りバカ・浜崎伝助氏は都心にある中堅の建設会社に勤務しております。 ② 伝助氏の住みかである公団の古いテラスハウスからの通勤時間は約一時間と少々…

Densuke's workplace is Sales Section 3 of the Sales Department. ③

① せっけいぶ 設計部　② けいりぶ 経理部　③ そして伝助氏の職場は営業部営業三課。　④ えいぎょうぶ 営業部　⑤ ぶちょう 部長　⑥ かちょう 課長　⑦ ヒラ

① ねえ　あとで銀座に出ない？　② うん　いいわよ。　③ ちょっとツモらないか？　④ 弱いくせに!!　知らないぞ　ハハハ…　⑤ ビビビーン！　⑥ プッ　⑦ えっ今夜ですか!?　⑧ すまんが頼むよ…　⑨ 急にスケジュールが空いたと連絡があったんだよ。　⑩ あの社長は忙しいヒトですからねえ…　⑪ 他の課長にと思ったんだがなにしろ先方さんはキミも知っての通り　有名な釣りキチだろ。　⑫ 我社で話についていけるのはキミをおいていないのだよ。

① キミの豊富な釣り知識を生かして…是非先方の新工場建設の契約を取ってきてくれ。 ② 努力してみます
ハイッ。 ③ ありがと… ④ うまくいけば僕も次期部長候補にキミを堂々と推せる!! 頼むよ佐々木君。
⑤ ハイ…!! ⑥ 鈴木君 鈴木君!! ⑦ キミ 鈴木君はどうした？ ⑧ はい!! K商事のコンペに招かれまし
て… ⑨ 熊谷君は？ ⑩ やはりコンペの方に… ⑪ チッコの大事なときに誰もいないなんてーっ…!! ⑫ コ
ホンッ!!

① しかたない‼ 浜崎君ついてきたまえ‼ ②ハイッ ③営業マンの条件は、如才なく、機転がきいて、手際のよいことだそうです。しかし、その条件を一番満たさない男が残っていたのです。 ④ハイヤーとは豪勢ですね なんスか 今日は？ ⑤大事な接待だよ。 ⑥そうスか ドーりで。 ⑦浜崎君‼ すべて僕が取り仕切るからキミは黙って僕の指示に従ってくれればいいからね。 ⑧どうも‼ その方が気楽でいいス。 ⑨課長『こういうチャンスにはみんな自分を必死で売り込もうとするのに、この男ときたらもうっ』 ⑩課長、最近釣りの方はどうです？ ⑪キミには上昇志向ってものはないのかね？ ⑫はあ？ ⑬つまりエラクなりたいって思うことだよ。 ⑭そりゃー僕だってその気はあるんじゃないスか。 ⑮女房もいつもエラクなって‼ エラクなって‼ と言ってるし… ⑯女房がねえ…

Yes, yes. I understand that. ②

These entities called "companies" are very cleverly set up, you see, making the employees compete by giving them ranks. They're designed so that the end result is business growth. ①

Section chief: *I wonder if he really does.* ③

Take me, for example—I don't want to advance so badly that I would kick others out of the way, but it would be humiliating to be outdone by others who entered the company at the same time as me. ⑥

Yes, sir! ⑤

Say, Driver, hurry it up. We're supposed to meet our client at 7:00. ④

Yes, yes. ⑧

That's the normal way for a person to feel, don't you think? ⑦

Ha ha ha! That's right, isn't it. ⑫

Idiot! That's because he skipped over group leader and went right to deputy section chief! ⑪

No, if I'm not mistaken, Tsuda hasn't become a group leader, has he? ⑩

You, on the other hand... I don't know whether to call you noble or what... You are the only person in your entering class who hasn't become a group leader yet. ⑨

①会社ってのは巧く出来ててね　社員にランクをつける事で競争させる…その結果業績も伸びるという仕組みになっているのだよ。　②分かる　分かる　分かりますよそれ。　③課長「こいつほんとに分かっているのかね？」　④ねっキミいそいでよ。七時に先方と待ち合わせてるんだから…　⑤ハイ！　⑥僕なんかも他人を蹴落としてまで偉くなりたいとは思わんが…同期の者に追い越されるのは口惜しい…　⑦それがごく普通の人間感情というものだろう？　⑧分かります分かります。　⑨そこいくとキミは立派というかなんというか…キミの同期で係長になってないのはキミだけなんだから…　⑩いや、たしか津田君が係長をやってなかった…んじゃないかな？　⑪バカ！　あれは係長を飛び越えて課長代理になったの!!　⑫ハハハ　そうでしたっけ。

① 浜崎！「ハハハ　そうでしたっけ」はないだろ。　② キミ…すまないネ。こんなにダラダラくだらん話をする気じゃなかったんだが…　③ い、いやそんな…　④ もうちょっとだけ言わせてくれな。　⑤ どーぞ。⑥ ウォッホン！　⑦ キミもコリ始めた釣りのように仕事にも欲が出ないのかね。　⑧ 課長!!　釣りと仕事とは比べもんにならないでしょ!?　⑨ 釣りには男のロマンがあるって言ったのは課長ですよ!!

① その釣りと仕事を比較するなんて!! ② アハハハハ… ③ 面白いヒトですね。 ④ 今どきのサラリーマン
には貴重な存在ですよ。 ⑤ 貴重な存在だって… ⑥ こりゃどーも。 ⑦ 課長「この男を釣りの世界へ引き
込んだことは、我が人生で最大のミステークとなるんじゃなかろうか…」

① きょうは忙しいところ時間をさいていただきましてどうも… ② いや なんのなんの。 ③ 心おきなくお
くつろぎください。 ④ 例の余興もちゃんと用意してありますから… ⑤ ほっ あれを!? ⑥ まあ社長さん
お久しぶりーっ!! ⑦ ではさっそく… ⑧ 食べやんせー 食べやんせー 食べよかな それともチョチョンと
からかって 遊ぼかなー ⑨ な、なんスかあれ!! ⑩ 釣り好きの社長が自分で作り出した遊びだよ。

① あそれそれ！ ② 食べやんせー ③ 食べよかな よそおかな ④ バッカみたい… ⑤ イジジジ ⑥ キミ、我々は接待係!! ⑦ はあ ⑧ この場をシラケさせたらおシマイだぞ。 ⑨ 佐々木君 ⑩ ハイッ ⑪ は よいしょ!! 食べよかね 食べずにチョンチョンと逃げよかね ⑫ ワッハッハ ⑬ あの無器用な課長が… ⑭ よーし 課長ひとりを道化にはしないス!!

① チョコンとアタリがありやした ② ハ、ヨイショ 食べよかなん ③ 食べずにチョチョンと逃げよかね ④ ワッハッハ ワッハッハ ⑤ 社長は上機嫌…自ら銀座に繰り出そうといい出しました。 ⑥ ワッハッハッハッハ… ⑦ イヤーッ愉快じゃった。 ⑧ と、ここまでの接待は大成功だったのですが…

① みなさん水割りで… ② すみません ぼくはビールを… ③ 薄くしてください。 ④ なあ、佐々木君…
⑤ ハイッ ⑥ キミはどう思うね? ⑦ と申しますと? ⑧ 釣りの本道は渓流釣りだなどという輩がおるが…
⑨ ハアハア おりますなあ… ⑩ すぐ行き止りの渓流で小魚などを釣って何が面白いんだろうね。 ⑪ ごもっ
ともです。 ⑫ ワシは釣りは海!! しかもトローリングに限ると思うんだがね。 ⑬ トローリング いいです
なあ… ⑭ チョットすまん みんなどいてっ!!

① 誰もいない広い海にクルーザーを疾走させる。 ② まっ青な空に積乱雲が勇壮に湧き昇る… ③ モクモクモク… ④ ワシはトローリングチェアに座り…白い航跡を見つめている。 ⑤ と、突然!! ⑥ "フィンノール"のリールが唸って "シェークスピア" のロッドが折れんばかりにしなる! ストライク（あたり）だ!! ⑦ やがて120パンドのバークレーの太いラインの向こうに… ⑧ 巨大なブルーマーリンの姿が!! 激しいテールウォーク

① 奴と私の壮絶なファイトが始まる！　②やがて空が夕日で赤く染まるころ…奴は力尽き　その巨体を私の前に横たえる…　③なるほどー。　④それでキミ　帰りのキャビンから陸の灯りを見やりながら乾杯するマルチーニは最高なんだ。　⑤本当の釣りってのはそれにふさわしい地位と教養が要求される、グレースフルなスポーツなんだよ。　⑥チッ　⑦ちょっと濃く作って…!!　⑧そこいくと乗り合いの釣り船はダメだねえ。

① 乗り合い船はギューギューにスシ詰めにされて…あれじゃラッシュアワーの電車だよ。 ② まるで山手線から釣り糸を垂らしてるみたいだ。 ③ ホホホ ④ うぬ〜っ ⑤ 社長、それはないでしょ!! ⑥ うん? ⑦ さっきから聞いてるとやれカルチャーとかグレースフルとかエラそーに!! ⑧ 釣りだけは身分に関係なくみんなが楽しめるもんなんス!! ⑨ 佐々木君!! ⑩ そうですよね課長!! ⑪ オンザロック!!

① なにが山手線から釣り糸ですか!! ② いったい自分を何様だと思っているんですか!! ③ 佐々木君 こいつを何とかしたまえ。 ④ はあ…お言葉ですが私もひとこと。 ⑤ なっ ⑥ なんだキミッ…!? ⑦ 社長。 ⑧ ど、どうしたんだ一体… ⑨ クルーザーでトローリングも愉しいでございましょう。 ⑩ キャビンで飲むマルチーニもおいしいでしょう。 ⑪ 分かればいい…分かれば!!

① 社長!! ② ハイッ ③ しかし…スシ詰めの船釣りにも愉しみがあるのです。 ④ 帰りの舟べりで飲むワン
カップの冷酒もマルチーニに負けずおいしいものです。 ⑤ ワンカップ冷酒万才!! ⑥ カミさんが作ってくれ
たオニギリもけっこううまいものです。 ⑦ 釣りにはそれぞれに愉しみが…詩があるのです。 ⑧ 課長　注
がせてください。 ⑨ うん… ⑩ 自分の釣りを自慢するのは構いません…しかし、他人の釣りまで悪くいう
のは同じく釣りを楽しむ仲間として許すことはできません! ⑪ 課長よく言った!

① 他人の釣りを認められない人は釣り人じゃない。そんなのはただのサカナ獲りです。　② ウギギー！　③ ブルーマーリンがなんだ　デカイのがいいんなら…　④ 捕鯨船に乗れ　ホゲイ船に！　⑤ うっうっうっ…!!　⑥ バカモン!!　⑦ ワシャ帰るぞ!!　⑧ 帰れ帰れ　ボケ社長!!　⑨ ワッハッハッハッハッハッ…　⑩ 清酒月星　やきとり神田川

①うめーっ　最高にうめえー!! ②ボカァ課長を見直したス　握手握手。　③やっぱり…いうべきじゃなかった
た…　④いや、本当の釣り師なら絶対にいうべきです！　⑤食べやんせー　食べやんせー　⑥食べよかな
それともチョンチョンとからかって遊ぼかな。　⑦バッカみたい　ハハハハハハ…　⑧わしはキミがうらやま
しいよ。　⑨なんでですか？　⑩そうやって明日のことを考えずに、言いたい事を言えるキミがね…

① 課長に責任はないスよ　あのボケが悪いんス!!　② 公衆便所　③ なにが乗り合い船はイカンですか。　④ な
にが山手線ですか。冗談言っちゃいけませんよーてんだ!!　⑤ ねえ課長　そうスよね!!　⑥ 帰ろうか…　⑦ 旅行
協会　国鉄　⑧ 過ぎたるは及ばざるがごとし。時間が経つにつれ　事の重大さに言葉も出ない二人でありまし
た。

① そして翌朝、いつもより一時間も早く出勤したふたりでありました。 ② 佐々木良介 浜崎伝助 悌次郎 美知子 志乃 正子 洋平 弘 ③ お早ようございます。 ④ …ヨッ ⑤ お早ようございまーす。 ⑥ お早 よース!! ⑦ 課長 お早ようございます。 ⑧ 浜崎さん お早よう!! ⑨ なによあのふたり…? ⑩ へーんな の。

① やあ諸君　お早よう。　② 佐々木君　ゆうべはご苦労さん!!　③ ハ、ハイ!!　④ さっそくあっちで報告を聞こうか?　⑤ ハイ　営業三課です。　⑥ アッ　⑦ モ、モ、モシモシ…　⑧ ヒッ　⑨ エッ

①そ、そんな…こちらこそ…　②は、はい！　ありがとうございます…　③け、契約<ruby>オーケイ<rt>けいやく</rt></ruby>だって…　④ゆうべのことをわざわざ<ruby>詫<rt>わ</rt></ruby>びてきた。<ruby>自分<rt>じぶん</rt></ruby>のわがままな<ruby>釣<rt>つ</rt></ruby>り<ruby>観<rt>かん</rt></ruby>を<ruby>直<rt>なお</rt></ruby>してくれたと、お<ruby>礼<rt>れい</rt></ruby>までいっていたよ。　⑤か、<ruby>課長<rt>かちょう</rt></ruby>!!　⑥ハマちゃん！　⑦<ruby>食<rt>く</rt></ruby>いやんせー　<ruby>食<rt>く</rt></ruby>いやんせー　<ruby>食<rt>た</rt></ruby>べよかな　それともチョチョイとからかって<ruby>遊<rt>あそ</rt></ruby>ぼかな　⑧キ、キミたちいったいどうしたのかね…？

3 Evolution of the Office Lady

Author & Artist: Risu Akizuki

Essay by Jeannie Lo

Omnipresent in Japan's company offices are young women making copies, faxing memos, typing correspondence, and performing a multitude of secretarial duties. These OLs, or Office Ladies, comprise the majority of all clerical workers in Japan. Their tasks generally require little mental challenge and seem to squander the years of studying and learning they have invested into getting through the Japanese educational system. Who are these OLs, and what are their motivations in the Japanese workforce?

OLs are the Girls Friday of the Japanese corporate world. Roles in a Japanese company, as in Japanese society, are typically predetermined; as the women in this group, OLs are expected to perform supportive and domestic roles. In addition to their secretarial duties, they make tea, serve snacks, clean the telephones every morning, and shop for gifts, supplies, and food. Japanese corporations have no qualms assigning such unchallenging tasks to OLs since they are expected to—and virtually always do—quit when they marry or start a family. Some Japanese corporations even nudge their young OLs into marriage by offering classes in sewing, cooking, flower arrangement, and other skills that will make them more attractive marriage prospects.

OLs are typically single and in their twenties, and they view their OL years as a time of freedom and independence to enjoy life, to travel to foreign countries, and to shop with abandon. Many live with their parents or in inexpensive company dormitories, allowing them the luxury of spending their paychecks on themselves. Typically, they use their income to pursue leisure interests before they marry and must cope with the daily pressures and responsibilities of family life.

In other words, the priorities of OLs do not lie in their work. Since they are on the *ippanshoku,* or "general," track (as opposed to the *sogoshoku,* or "integrated," career track), promotions are unlikely even with a consistently stellar job performance. Consequently, unless there are deadlines or other extenuating circumstances, OLs can leave the office when the workday officially ends. By contrast, their male co-workers, the "salarymen," are expected to perform *zangyō* ("overtime work") every night.

Lacking a strong commitment to the corporation and not yet saddled with family responsibilities, OLs tend to spend a significant amount of time playing. Indeed, life for the average OL starts "after 5." Once the workday ends, OLs often leave together to shop or to eat at fashionable restaurants frequented by young twenty-somethings. On Friday nights, they may undergo a complete metamorphosis in the ladies' locker room before leaving work. Removing their conservative office attire, they put on flashier clothes and makeup to dance the night away at trendy discos. Their main priority is to enjoy their lives while they can as young single adults with few responsibilities.

While at the company and under the watchful eyes of bosses, however, OLs are strictly professional beings. Corporate expectations of them are very clearly defined and practiced in training sessions for new employees. In classes and in the manuals they receive, OLs are instructed in the minutiae of proper business behavior. They learn such things as how deeply to bow in various situations, the specific phrases to use when receiving company calls, the proper way to make tea, and the correct imperturbable Zen-like demeanor to adopt when working at the reception desk.

While OLs may not derive great satisfaction from the content of their work, they are generally quite happy not to be on the career track. They shun the heavy personal sacrifices that salarymen must make to the company as they build their careers. Boredom with their work, shared annoyance at male co-workers, and similar life and leisure interests are the glue that bonds OLs in lasting and sometimes lifelong friendships. In the company of other OLs, these women can present their honest feelings and true selves. The office OL group is a strong sisterhood of women who eat their lunches and enjoy leisure activities together, socializing both inside and outside of the company.

The sisterhood of OLs also functions as an informal support group, helping these well-educated women put up with the boredom of mindless work and, not infrequently, with the undesirable behavior of certain men in the office. This behavior can range from authoritarian self-centeredness to sexual harassment. Since complaining publicly would disturb the harmony of the workgroup, OLs will instead seek comfort from other women in the same predicament.

On the other hand, it is not uncommon to find an OL turning the attention of male co-workers to her benefit by playing the part of a *burriko*—that is, acting like a little girl and feigning physical weakness and helplessness. This form of flirtation is often effective in manipulating and eliciting the help of men in the office. It may also endear them to bosses who will feel sorry for them and lighten their workload, resulting in more time and energy for their "after 5" leisure activities.

Flirtation can also help OLs in the not uncommon practice of finding fiancés among the ranks of salarymen at their company. Romance within the company must be conducted in secret to avoid company gossip and maintain an air of propriety in front of management, which is often shielded from the private lives of employees. If the OL is lucky, such courtship may lead to the achievement of a "goal-in." In other words, she will marry, quit her job, and leave the tedium of clerical responsibilities. At that point, she will also leave the fun of her OL days and move on to her next station in life, as a housewife, mother, and perhaps a part-time worker.

Let Me Tell You ①　　　The Professional ①

① ほかでもない ② 単調な仕事だねえ あきない？
③ いえ わりと向いてるみたいです ④ 前は営業事務
やってたんですけど電話やら連絡やらめまぐるしくて
⑤ あたしトロいからミスばっかりしてました ⑥ この
仕事なら私でも役に立つんだなーって思えて ⑦ うれ
しくって ⑧ 単調な仕事はいやだのあきただの言う
連中に聞かせてやりたかったですよ ⑨ うちでいちば

ん言うのはおまえだぞ

---

① プロフェッショナル ② お茶でもどう？ダメ？
③ 電話番号教えてよ ねー ④ あっ鈴木保奈美に似て
る‼ ⑤ ボッ ⑥ だめ ⑦ すいませーん ⑧ 受付業務
実務講座

69

I'm Sorry ①　　　One of the Girls ①

I'm sorry. I'll do it right away. ③

Have you made the copies I asked for? ②

That girl from the temp service really works hard, doesn't she. ②

I'm sorry. I'll have it for you by the end of the day. ⑤

Do you have the results of the data from yesterday? ④

Oh, thank you very much. I'd love to. ④

Why don't you come work for us full time? ③

Yes, sir. I'm sorry. ⑦

Say... ⑥

Now she's just like our other OLs. ⑤

Potato Chips ⑥

Oh! Right. I mean... I'm sorry. ⑨

But I haven't asked you anything yet. ⑧

All the temps are like that. ⑧

Before, I didn't have anybody to talk to, and all I did was work! ⑦

hee hee hee

① スイマセン ② さっき頼んだコピーは？ ③ スイマセーン　すぐやります ④ きのうのデータの集計は？ ⑤ スイマセーン　今日中には ⑥ あのね ⑦ はあい　スイマセーン ⑧ まだ何も言ってないけど ⑨ あっ　はいあの　すいませんっ

① 仲間入り ② 派遣会社から来たコ　よく働くねえ ③ うちの正社員になりませんか？ ④ はいっ　ありがとうございます ⑤ 他のOLと同じになってしまった ⑥ ポテトチップス ⑦ 昔はね　おしゃべりする相手がいなくて仕事ばっかりしてたのよー ⑧ 派遣のコってみんなそうよねー

70

A Call From Mom ①

Mr. Yamakawa is not in right now. Would you like to leave a message? ③

Is Mr. Yamakawa in? ②

Thank you for all your kindness. Mr. Yamakawa is not in his office. How can I be of assistance? ⑤

This is Mrs. Yamakawa. I wonder if my husband is in? ④

I'll have him return your call later. ⑦

I'm very much obliged. Is that so? ⑥

Already? I was having fun. ⑨

Thanks, Mom. That's okay for now. ⑧

Sound Asleep ①

Uh-huh. ③

You spread out the papers like this. ②

And when you're sleepy, you pretend like you're reading them and you take a nap. ④

Zzzz Zzzz

....

① 親子：でんわ ② あのー山川さんいらっしゃいますか？ ③ 山川はただいま外出中です。ご伝言がございましたらうけたまわりますが… ④ 山川の家内ですけど主人はおりますでしょうか ⑤ いつもお世話になっております　山川は外出中ですがいかがいたしましょう ⑥ オソレいります　サヨウでございますか

⑦ 後ほどこちらからお電話いたします ⑧ ありがとお母さん　もういいよ ⑨ なんだ　けっこーおもしろかったのに ⑩ OLのマナー

---

① ぐっすり ② こうやって書類を広げるでしょ ③ ハイ ④ 眠い時は読んでるふりしていねむりするのよ

71

A Woman with Two Faces ①

You'll get used to this kind of work before too long. ④

That's okay. I'll do half of it for you. ③

I'm sorry. I haven't finished it yet. ②

But I've heard that she's an entirely different person around men. ⑥

She's really friendly and outgoing, isn't she. ⑤

No, it's not like that. ⑨

Really? ✿ Oh my! ⑧

Whaat?! You mean she acts like a ditz? ⑦

She's gone to only girls' schools, and it seems she still isn't used to dealing with men. ⑫

RATTLE

SHAKE

Y—yes, sir. ⑪

Okay, do these like the others. ⑩

....

Paid Vacation ①

I'd like to take tomorrow morning off. ②

I have something urgent to take care of tomorrow, so I'd like to leave around noon. ③

?

What's up with everyone? ④

Aha! ⑤

BIG SALE

50% OFF

Starts Tomorrow ⑥

① 表裏のある女 ② すいません　まだできてなくって…③ いいよ　半分やってあげる ④ こんなのそのうち慣れるからねっ⑤ あの先輩気さくでいい人ね⑥ でもさー男の前じゃ別人みたいになるって話よ⑦ えーっ!?　あの人がブリッコするの？ ⑧ えー　やだー ⑨ いやそうじゃなくって ⑩ じゃあこれいつも

のように⑪ ハ　ハイッ⑫ ずっと女子校でいまだに免疫ないらしいの

___

① 有給休暇 ② 明日午前中ちょっと休みたいんですが③ 明日急用があるので午後から出社します④ なんだみんなで⑤ あ⑥ グランドバーゲン　明日から

Unwitting Revenge ①

Hey! Get me some tea! ②

Y-yes, sir. ③

Well, it's part of the job, I guess. ⑤

The boss has a lot of nerve asking you to make tea when we're so busy. ④

Huh? ⑦

So you say, while secretly taking revenge. You're pretty sneaky, aren't you. Heh heh heh. ⑥

I've been using it all along to clean cups!! ⑨

Whaat?! This is a dust rag?! ⑧

Whaat?

Reiko, the President's Secretary ①

Yes, sir. ③

You go on up the elevator. I'll take the stairs. ②

Boo-hoo

Ah!

Ah!

No. Well, actually... I guess it did. ⑤

Did it tire you out? ④

① 知らぬが悪魔 ②きみ お茶 ③は はい ④この忙しいのに部長にも困ったもんね ⑤まあこれも仕事のうちだから ⑥とか言ってだまってしかえしするなんてあんたもやるじゃないの　うふふ… ⑦え？ ⑧これぞーきんなの？ ⑨ずっと使ってたわよ　あたしっ

① 社長秘書　玲子 ②キミはエレベーターで上がりなさい　私は階段を使うから ③はい ④お疲れですか？ ⑥いや…まあそうだね

Fight or Flight ①   Chameleon ①

① 闘う女闘えない女 ② おっ元気？ ③ いやあん　や
めてくださあい ④ あのねー　あなたがああいう態度
とると女子社員みんなにとってよくないと思うのよ
⑤ …はあ ⑥ あなただってほんとはイヤなんでしょ
本気で笑ってるわけじゃないでしょ ⑦ はい…でも…
あの…⑧ 私ってーなあんかイヤな目にあうと笑って

逃げちゃうんですよお

———————————————

① カメレオン ② 暗いよな　あのコ ③ バカ　聞こえ
るぜ ④ 何とでも言えばいいわ　お茶くみOLは仮の姿
⑤ ほんとうの私は… ⑥ さあ ⑦ ライブ行くぞっ
⑧ やっぱり目立たない ⑨ ライブハウスM

The Last One ①

The Conspirators ①

① 最後の一人 ② できました ③ はいごくろうさん ④ できました ⑤ 私も ⑥ はいはい 遅くまで悪かったね ⑦ じゃーお先にー ⑧ だいじょうぶ？ ⑨ はい ⑩ 子どものころにもよくこういうことがありましたから ⑪ 手伝う 手伝う

① なれあう二人 ② 受付 ③ ねえ3時からちょっと出てきていいかな ④ うん ⑤ そのかわり金曜は5時に帰らせてね ⑥ デートね いいわよ ⑦ 最初は気が合わなくてどうなるかと思ったけど ⑧ よく話してみるといいコじゃない ⑨ そろそろ配置がえの時期ね

Timing ①

Visiting the Company ①

① タイミング ② できたっ！今日は早いっ ③ ん？
④ えっ会議明日の９時？困ったな 資料、間にあうか
な ⑤ いかーん　今行くとあの仕事で残業だあ ⑥ 困っ
たなーも─… ⑦ あれ今日の分は？ ⑧ まだ？ ⑨ 残業
いちばん遅い人のもの

① 会社訪問 ② では失礼します ③ 人事部 ④ 近頃の学生
はリッチだねー　イタリア製の背広なんか着てるや
つもいるんだ ⑤ はあそうですか ⑥ 気にいらんね
⑦ 断じて気にいらん ⑧ 来年はかっこいい男の子が
入ってきたらいいねー ⑨ 望み薄だよ

76

Fractions ①

Let's see... 18.94 ③

What's 360 divided by 19? ②

Bummer. ⑤

It's a fraction, huh. ④

360 divided by 18 is exactly 20, isn't it! ⑧

Oh! It's 18 people, then. ⑦

I don't want any, so... ⑥

Who brought a round cake, of all things? ⑩

Well, then, I'll divide it up. ⑨

News to Me ①

What??!! ③

It's been decided that in order to conserve energy, heat in the building will be kept down. ②

And from now on it will be acceptable for female employees to wear sweaters over their uniforms, to wear heavy tights, and to use a blanket to cover their knees. ④

Chief! You mean... ⑤

So it seems... ⑦

...that was all prohibited until now? ⑥

① 端数 ② 360割る19っていくつ？ ③ えーとね 18。94
④ ハンパだなー ⑤ 困ったねー ⑥ ワタシはいらないか
ら ⑦ あっ じゃあ18人だから ⑧ 360割る18でちょう
ど20ね ⑨ では分けるぞ ⑩ だれだ 丸いケーキなんか
持ってきたの

① 初耳 ② 省エネのため暖房をすこしひかえることに
なった ③ えーっ!? ④ で これからは女子社員は制服
の上にセーターを着たり厚いタイツをはいたりひざ
かけ毛布を使ったりしてもよいということだ
⑤ 課長！それじゃあ ⑥ 今までは禁止されてたんです
かぁ？⑦ そうみたいだな

When your Lifestyle Changes ①

> What?! When did you two...? ③

> We're getting married. ②

> She's a real go-getter, huh. ⑥

> She hooked him in three months. ⑤

> They say *she* went after *him*. ④

> Come on, it wasn't anything serious. ⑧

> That's too bad. You liked him too, didn't you... ⑦

> It's gotten to her. ⑪

> I've decided to eat my favorite food first. ⑩

> Huh? You always eat the omelet last! ⑨

I Hate It When It's Nice ①

> How's the weather? ③

> If you don't hurry, you'll be late. ②

> Oh no. ⑤

> Fine!! It's a great day. ④

> Well, if the weather is bad, it's no problem, but... ⑦

> What? Is going to work on the weekend so tough? ⑥

> Aah, what a nice day. ⑧

> darn

> shoot

---

① 生きかたが変わる時 ② ぼくたち結婚します ③ えーっ!? いつの間にお前ら ④ 彼女からアタックしたんだって ⑤ ３ヵ月でゴールインか ⑥ やるわねー ⑦ 残念だったね あんたも彼のこと… ⑧ いやね そんなマジじゃなかったのよ ⑨ あれ？いつもは卵焼き最後でしょ ⑩ 好物は先に食べることにしたのっ ⑪ こたえ

てるじゃん

---

① 晴れたら やだな ② 早くしないと遅刻するわよ ③ …天気はどーだ ④ 快晴!! きもちいいわよ ⑤ あーあ ⑥ なによ 休日出勤そんなにつらいの？ ⑦ いやー 天気が悪けりゃ楽なんだけど… ⑧ あーっ なあんていい天気なんだっ

Director Hira Namijirō

Author & Artist: Tatsuo Nitta

Essay by Glen S. Fukushima

This selection from *Director Hira Namijirō* offers an amusing look at one of the most contentious and persistent trade issues between the United States and Japan over the past 20 years—automobiles and automobile parts.

These two sectors constitute approximately two-thirds of the $65 billion trade deficit the U.S. had with Japan in 1994. American cars account for less than two percent of the Japanese market, whereas Japanese cars account for 24 percent of the U.S. market. Although Japanese often claim that European cars have had much more success in Japan than American cars, total car imports account for only 4.6 percent of the Japanese market, in contrast to the 33 to 57 percent import share in the other G-7 countries. The imbalance in auto parts trade is even more dramatic—2.6 percent imports in Japan versus 16 to 60 percent imports in the other G-7 countries.

The story that follows depicts the two sides of the debate—American and Japanese—in a stereotyped and polarized fashion. Chairman Icepocca of Chrosler (i.e., former Chairman Iacocca of Chrysler Corporation) is shown to be a stereotypical American business leader: large, domineering, dogmatic, emotional, short-tempered, belligerent, and—until the end of the story—unreasonable and adversarial.

The Japanese business leaders—Chairman Chūsuke Arai and President and CEO Tatsuzō Saotome of Daitoku Automobile Corporation—are depicted as equally unsavory in their own way. They are imperious, hypocritical, self-centered, emotional, finger-pointing, spineless company men who attempt to foist off unpleasant tasks—such as dealing with boisterous foreigners like Icepocca—on subordinates like Hira.

Hira ends up as the only honest, reasonable, and objective male in this story. He is the only one who is able to explain dispassionately both to Icepocca how the Japanese side sees the U.S.-Japan auto trade dispute and to Arai and Saotome how the American side views the situation. As someone who understands and explains both sides, Hira is also the subject of criticism and accusations by both.

In addition to the depiction of the personalities of the two sides, it should also be noted that the characteristics of American and Japanese cars are stereotyped: as for the former, as Icepocca boasts during his drunken evening performance, "It accelerates! It corners! It stops!" Further, "when it comes to power, you can't beat an American car!" But Hira has the last word: "Even when treated so roughly, Japanese cars don't break down."

The fundamental issue being debated here is the cause of the huge U.S.-Japan trade imbalance in autos and auto parts. From the Japanese perspective, the cause is simple: Japanese cars are more competitive than American cars. This is largely the result of "quality control"—building high quality cars and selling them at low prices. This is the explanation that Hira offers Icepocca at dinner and the response Arai and Saotome give Hira at the end of the story.

Icepocca's interpretation is quite different. The Japanese trade surplus in autos and auto parts is a result of "unfair trade practices." This includes unnecessarily meticulous inspections of imported American cars by Japanese bureaucrats for the purpose of limiting the number of cars on Japanese roads. It also includes business practices: "How can we expect to compete on an equal footing with cars made in a country where they work 2,200 hours a year, damn it!"

Hira's view takes both interpretations into account. He tells Icepocca over dinner, "Until now we've maintained the view that there can be nothing wrong with selling cheap cars that perform well, but we're starting to think that this view has perhaps grown outdated." He also mentions that Japanese purchasing behavior is influenced by "pressure from MITI"—corroborating Icepocca's suspicion of Japanese government intervention to keep American autos and parts out of Japan. Note, however, that the Japanese auto industry sees the Japanese government's stance on trade issues as weak-kneed; Chairman Arai says of President Saotome: "Is he attempting kowtow diplomacy, just like our spineless government?" At the very end of the manga, Hira elaborates on why Japan is "able to make good products cheaply. It's because our method of setting prices is different. We should compete in the marketplace at prices that fully reflect social costs and benefits, as American companies do."

Hira's interpretation of what Icepocca really wants is interesting. Although Icepocca is ostensibly asking for Japanese auto companies to buy more American auto parts and for Japanese consumers to buy more American automobiles, Hira says, "It's not that they want us to buy American cars and car parts. They just want us not to sell any more Japanese cars in America than we already are."

This illustrates a major theme in U.S.-Japan trade conflict over the past 30 years. The issue, simply put, is this: The U.S. government, based on its free trade ideology and value placed on consumer sovereignty, would prefer to open Japan's markets to American products rather than to close the U.S. market to Japanese products, since this is considered to distort the operation of free markets, to restrict trade, to give potential windfall profits to American firms, and to deprive American consumers of products they would otherwise buy.

American companies and labor unions would also like to see Japan's markets open up so as to provide "fair" competition, corporate revenues, and employment for American workers. But when faced with limited prospects of truly opening the Japanese market, they have sometimes opted for a second-best solution, which is to limit Japanese exports to the U.S. This almost came to pass in June of 1995, when the U.S. government was about to impose tariffs of $5.9 billion on 13 models of Japanese luxury cars. A last-minute settlement averted this action, but the agreement reached was so ambiguous that it almost guaranteed continued U.S.-Japan friction over autos and auto parts.

The Feel of an American Car

アメ車の乗り心地

I'd like to talk to you about quality control. ①

Quality control? ②

—though, it is true, exposing defects in the cars your co-workers have built can be painful. ④

I'm talking about certain special efforts a company has to make. In our company we have something called "factory commendations": the workers examine our cars down to the tiniest detail, and we award commendations to those who discover defects— ③

① 私がお聞き願いたいのは、品質管理のことです。　②ヒンシツカンリ？　③企業努力のことですよ。私どもでは工場表彰というのがあって、工場で車の細部にいたるまで検討し、欠陥を発見した者は表彰するんです
④ 仲間の造った車の欠陥を暴くというのは、本当に辛いものがありますけど…

The problem lies first of all in Japan's unfair trade practices! With all the inspections demanded by bureaucrats, American cars have to pass through 36 different people's hands before they can be driven on Japanese roads! ④

I see. That's why not even a single bolt is left untightened on a Japanese car. ①

Especially since there's pressure from MITI. ③

If the quality of your product is high, we'll buy it without even being asked. ②

This is bad. He's getting a dangerous look in his eye... ⑧

How can we expect to compete on an equal footing with cars made in a country where they work 2,200 hours a year, damn it!! ⑦

hic!

Uh-oh! ⑥

More sake! ⑤

① ナルホド…ソレデ日本車ハボルト一本ノ締メ忘レモナイワケダ… ② クォリティの高い製品なら頼まれなくても買いますよ。 ③ 通産省の圧力もございますし… ④ ソモソモ問題ハ日本ノアンフェアーナ通商システムニアル!! 米国車ガ日本ノ道路ヲ走レルヨウニナルマデ、役人ドモノ検査デナント36人ノ人ノ手ヲ経ナケリャナランノダゾ!! ⑤ モット酒! ⑥ あ… ⑦ 年間2200時間モ働ク国デ造ラレタ車ト対等ニ戦エルカ! バーロー!! ⑧ まずいな! 目がすわってきたよ…

① 私どもも、安くて性能の良い車を売って何が悪いという、これまでの考えではダメだと…　② オーッノー！
③ ワタシ逃ゲマース！　会長ノ車ニ乗リタクアリマセーン‼　④ 会長の車？

① カモン、ナミジロウ‼ ② 乗リナサイ‼ ③ そ、そんな…会長のお背中に乗るなんて… ④ 車とはコレの
ことか… ⑤ アメ車ニハ乗レンノカ‼ ⑥ じゃ、ちょっと麻布まで。

① パタパタ　② 会長　速過ぎますよ！　ストップ…　③ キキィッ!!

① ヒイッ!! ② オー! アイムソーリー。 ③ アメ車ハブレーキガヨク効キマスネ。次ハ気ヲツケマース。
④ モウダメ! 会長ハ酔ウト止マラナイ… ⑤ ゴオオオオオオン!! ⑥ キャーッ!!

① 急カーブ!! ② ワハハハハ…走ル! 曲ガル! 止マル! コノ基本性能ガアメ車ハグッドネ!! ③ 何をな
さっているんです!! ④ あ! ⑤ ブルルン! ブルルルル…

① アイスポッカ会長、お車に乗せていただくのは私のはずですが…

① ああ…!!　② リバース!!

① ハハハハッ！ アメ車ハパワーモ最高ネ!! ② 早ク救急車ヲ呼ビナサイ！ 骨折程度ナラヨイガ… ③ 平
取締役!! ④ オー、会長！ 何人病院送リニスルンデスカ!! ⑤ か…会長…

91

① これだけ乱暴な扱いをされてもですねえ…

Japanese cars don't break down. ①

① 日本の車(ジャパニーズカー)は故障しないんですよ。

The next morning...

DIRECTOR HIRA NAMIJIRO ①

Ouch... ②

Ah, it was nothing, ha ha ha... ⑤

I was waiting in the next room and heard an incredible noise. ④

Director Hira, what really happened during your dinner last night? ③

① 取締役平並次郎　② アタタタ…　③ 平取締役、昨夜の商談中本当は何があったんですか？　④ 控えの間で
お待ちしていたら、すごい音がしていましたが…　⑤ いやあ何でもないよ、ハハハ…

① とぼけちゃって…！　② どうせ応対がまずくて、アイスポッカ会長にぶん殴られたに決まってるわ。　③ 頼まれてた米国自動車業界の資料です。　④ ありがとう。　⑤ じゃ、私は秘書室へ戻りますので。　⑥ ん。　⑦ ここまでくると同情しちゃうわ。　⑧ 何かの間違いで取締役になったとはいえ、この人が引導を渡されるまではちゃんとご奉公するか…

① 社長室　② 前年比１０％の減益か…　③ 何なんだ、この最近の国内での販売の落ち込みは‼　④ やはりバブル崩壊と車庫法の改正による買い控えのせいかと…　⑤ 社長、平取締役が見えられました。

I've come to report on my meeting last night with Chairman Icepocca. ①

Looking at your face, I can see just what sort of meeting you had. ③

I don't need a report...You may leave. ②

Ha ha ha ha

Ah ha ha ha ha ha ha! ④

Ha ha ha ha

①昨夜_{さくや}のアイスポッカ会長_{かいちょう}との話_{はな}し合_あいの報告_{ほうこく}に参_{まい}りました。　②そんなものは聞_きくまでもない…下_さがりたまえ。　③その顔_{かお}をみれば、アイスポッカとどういう話_{はな}し合_あいをしたか分_わかるよ。　④グワッハッハッハッ。

97

① キッ

American-made auto parts ①

① 米国製の自動車部品

① ナミジロウハドコダ‼

Namijirō!! ①

This is terrible! ③

It's Chairman Icepocca! And he's shouting for Director Hira! ②

What?! Icepocca's here?! And he's scattering American car parts in the halls?! ④

① ナミジロウ!! ② アイスポッカ会長だわ! 平取締役の名を呼んでいる!! ③ 大変だ!! ④ 何ィ〜っ!! アイスポッカが廊下に米国製の自動車部品をバラまきながら来たあ!?

① 酔っとるのか!? ② そのようには見受けられませんが… ③ 社長も会うようですし、会長も会われるしか ないでしょう… ④ 応接室 ⑤ ハローアイスポッカ会長、お久しぶりです。

① うっ！　② ああ…つつ…　③ ナミジロウハドコダ!!　④ 平取締役　逃げて下さい!!　⑤ 取締役平並次郎
⑥ なんで私が逃げなきゃならないのかね？　⑦ 「氷のポッカ」と言われるアイスポッカ氏ですよ。　⑧ 平
取締役の名を叫んでいました。きっと昨夜の応対をまだ怒っているんですわ…今度こそ大ケガさせられますわ
よ！

① 何だ、アイスポッカ会長が来られたんですか。　②ハイ、平…あっ、片梨常務！　③すぐ20Fの応接室へ来い!!　④貴様、昨夜アイスポッカにどういう応対をしたんだ！　社長の手が握りつぶされるぞ!!　⑤は？
⑥アイスポッカ会長が…分かりました、すぐ参ります。　⑦これだけ言っても行くわけですか!!

① アイスポッカ会長はいい人だよ。② ダメだこりゃ！　面倒みきれないわもう…　③ 何をしとるんだ、社長のヤツは？　④ 弱腰の日本政府と同じように土下座外交しとるのか？　⑤ 会長、社長は実に情けない姿ですなあ。

① アイスポッカ会長、荒井です。　② ホホウ!!　ホホウ!!　③ オ、オヤジさん!!　④ ハー!!　ハー!!　ハー!!
⑤ アイスポッカ会長！

① オオッ!! ナミジロウ大丈夫デスカ!? ② ハロルドカラ聞イタヨ…昨夜ハ酔ッテ私ノ悪イ癖ガ出タヨウデスネ… ③ 今日ハナミジロウニ謝罪ニ来タンダ、本当ニゴメンナサイネ。 ④ 社長ト会長ハ卑怯ネ! 大事ナ問題ヲアナター人ニ任セテ…チョットコラシメテヤッタヨ! ⑤ うっ!!

Ahhhhh!!
①

I shouldn't have, Namijirō. So sorry. ④

Are you still drunk? ②

I can endure myself being roughed up. However, Arai and Saotome are the very embodiment of Daitoku Auto. I can't condone any behavior that is an affront to them. ③

① オオオオ〜!!　② まだ酔っておられるんですか。　③ 私が乱暴を受けるのは我慢いたします。しかしながら、荒井と早乙女はイコール「大徳自動車」です。それを足げにするようなマネ、見過ごすことはできません。　④ 悪カッタナミジロウ…ゴメンチャイ。

① どーもすいませんねえ、バカ力なもんで…　② ナミジロウ、モウ部品買ッテクレトセコイコトハ言ワヌ。堂々ト高品質ノ車デ勝負スルゾ！　③ 先ほど資料を見ましたが、衰えているといわれる米国のビッグ3は着々とリストラ（立て直し）を進め、回復しているようですね。　④ ナミジロウ、ユーハサムライネ。　⑤ シーユーアゲイン！

① 氷ではなく、愛すべきアイスポッカ氏なわけですよ。　② 社長、それに会長、彼らの本音はアメ車やその部品を買ってくれということじゃないんですよ。

① もうこれ以上、アメリカでは日本車を売ってくれるなと言うことです。　② なぜ日本は良い製品を安く造ることができるのか？　③ それは、価格設定の仕方が違うからです。アメリカのように社会的コスト、利益をちゃんと反映させた「価格」で市場競争すべきなんです。　④ 世界中を日本の車で埋めつくすおつもりですか？　⑤ 一体、どこまでもうければ気がすむんでしょう…

111

① き、貴様〜、それが経営に携わる取締役の言葉か！！ ② いいモノを安く造って売ることのどこが悪い?! ③ お前はどっちの味方だ?! ④ クビ覚悟の一ヒラ取のザレ事とお聞き流し下さい。 ⑤ 取締役、よくまあご無事で... ⑥ ねぇ...ハハハ。

Section Chief Kōsaku Shima

Author & Artist: Kenshi Hirokane

Essay by T. R. Reid

On a spring day in 1992, a fortyish salaryman at Hatsushiba Electric Co. was promoted from *kachō*, or "section chief," to the considerably more exalted post of *buchō*, or "division chief." Normally, that would be no big deal—it happens every spring at hundreds of Japanese companies. But this particular personnel change was treated as a significant news event in the national media. The *Mainichi Shimbun*'s headline captured the story: "Japan's Most Famous Salaryman Gets Promoted."

The salaryman in question, Kōsaku Shima, was actually a fictional character; his company, "Hatsushiba," was equally fictional. But there was nothing make-believe about that headline. Section Chief Shima has in fact become the archetype of the salaryman, the hard-working, hard-drinking junior executive who fights a never-ending battle for truth, profits, and the Japanese way.

As the title character of the enormously successful manga series *Section Chief Kōsaku Shima*, Shima is a ubiquitous figure in Japan. He is the subject of one full-length movie and a recurring series of TV dramas. His boyish but earnest face is used to advertise a variety of business-related products, from telephones to air travel. He has offered advice to his fellow junior executives in a series of non-fiction books, every one a bestseller. Meanwhile, the 17 volumes of paperback books, or *tankōbon*, derived from the series have sold more than 13 million copies.

Why? The main reason is the sheer narrative appeal of the Shima saga, a richly complex fabric of corporate intrigue, marketing savvy, and factional infighting. Time and again, our man Shima has to use all his ingenuity and strength to help Hatsushiba hold its own against Japanese and American competitors. And that's only the daytime half of the tale; Shima also finds the energy for a dizzying round of romantic adventures with attractive, and often sexually voracious, women.

It is not lost on anybody in Japan's business world that the fictional "Hatsushiba" is modeled on a real-life corporate giant, Matsushita, the huge consumer-electronics multinational firm that produces Panasonic, National, and other familiar brands. Many of the central plot twists in the "Hatsushiba" story—including the successful introduction of a home bread-making machine, as related in the excerpt that follows—are drawn from actual happenings at Matsushita.

The similarity is no surprise, because the creator of the series, Kenshi Hirokane, worked for three years as a salaryman at none other than Matsushita. Hirokane, a friendly but serious man in his late 40s with a raffish Clark Gable mustache, says he was never really comfortable in the corridors of a giant corporation. He dreamed of the day he could make his living as a *manga-ka*, a creator of manga.

Talk about dreams coming true! Today Hirokane is one of the best-known *manga-ka* in all Japan—although he's still nowhere near as famous as the section chief he created.

In Kōsaku Shima, Hirokane has created the paradigm of the *shigoto ningen*, the salaryman who basically lives for the job. As is common for corporate employees in Japan, our man Shima sees himself not so much as a sales type or an accountant or a manufacturing engineer; rather, he draws his identity from Hatsushiba. He goes where the company sends him, and puts his all into every assignment.

This kind of transition accounts for much of the tension in the excerpt that follows. After 18 years at Hatsushiba, Shima has run afoul of a factional dispute in the company's Tokyo offices, and found himself shipped off to a manufacturing plant in Kyoto. His approach to the new post fits the idealized notion of what a good salaryman should do. If you know nothing about manufacturing, then it's your duty to knuckle down and learn. If you don't like bread, you'd better eat bread day after day after day until you grow to like it.

Section Chief Shima's core faith is that a little ingenuity and a lot of hard work can solve any problem. And solving problems for the advancement of Hatsushiba Corp. is basically what the section chief's life is all about.

Shima's promotion from section chief to division chief in 1992 marked the end of the 13-year-long manga series. "Enough is enough," Hirokane said then, as he put Shima and Hatsushiba out to pasture. "I want to put my energy into something new."

And yet, even without the powerful platform of a weekly manga series, Kōsaku Shima has survived—indeed thrived—as an icon of contemporary pop culture. Every year he shows up in more TV commercials. Every year new volumes in the non-fiction series "Kōsaku Shima's Formula for Success" are published. As a result, Section Chief Shima remains the exemplar of his type—the hard-charging, no-nonsense company man who built Japan into a global economic superpower. It is a type that remains immensely popular and influential in Japan.

In the spring of 1995, NHK's Sunday morning show *Keizai Scope* arranged a debate pitting two styles of salaryman against one another. In one corner was Hirokane, representing Section Chief Shima and other earnest, hard-working *shigoto ningen*. In the other was Jūzō Yamasaki, creator of the beloved "Hama-chan," the laid-back hero of the manga series *Diary of a Fishing Freak*.

Hirokane presented the case for hard work. Yamazaki presented the case for going fishing. The moderator and the studio audience, comprising 50 male and female executives from major companies, were asked to choose the winner.

The result was a landslide: these real-life salarymen and career women declared by more than a two to one margin that they would prefer to emulate Kōsaku Shima, still the paradigm of the hard-working company man—and still Japan's most famous salaryman.

① Morning starts early at the Kyoto factory. All employees participate in radio calisthenics just before 8 AM.

② A-One Two Three Four...

Safety First

④ One: Service to Society.

③ The morning meeting that follows begins with a recitation in unison of "The Five Principles" set forth by founder Hatsutarō Yoshiwara.

⑥ The crew at the head office were generally critical of this recitation of "The Five Principles," a sort of brainwashing device like the quotations of Chairman Mao during the Cultural Revolution in China...

⑤ One: Service to Society!

① 京都工場の朝は早い 従業員は8時前のラジオ体操に全員参加する ② おいっちにいさんしい ③ その後行われる朝礼は創始者 吉原初太郎の唱えた "五つの精神" を唱和することから始まる ④ 一つ、社会奉仕の精神 ⑤ ひとつ、しゃかいほうしのせいしん ⑥ 中国文革時代の毛語録のような洗脳効果を期待するこの五精神唱和に本社の連中はおおむね批判的であったが…

The people here, however, are surprisingly cooperative, and take it very seriously. ①

Such earnestness was completely lacking among those at the head office—especially among those of us in the Advertising Department. ②

It's been a whole week since I arrived at my new workplace, but people in my section still haven't quite warmed up to me. I feel a strange sense of isolation. ③

①こっちの連中はおどろくほど素直で真剣だ… ②この真面目さは 本社の とりわけ我々宣伝部の連中には 皆無であった ③新しい職場へ来て1週間にもなるが 課の人間がいまいちうちとけてこない 俺は妙な孤立 感を味わっている…

Perhaps it is just that the custom of excluding newcomers still lingers in Kyoto. ①

Perhaps the cliquishness of Gion teahouses extends throughout the entire city. ②

The female employees are especially cold and distant. It must be my rash comment the other day about the bread they had made. ④

No, that's not it. ③

This bread isn't very good, is it. We should assemble some experts and have them come up with some tastier breads. ⑤

I'll bet nasty rumors about me have spread among all the girls in the office, and Suzukamo has heard them, too. ⑧

Click
Click

Your tea, sir. ⑦

Tunk!

Even Suzukamo in my section seems distant somehow. ⑥

① やはり京都は一見さんお断りの習俗が残っているんだろうか… ② この排他的なところは祇園の世界と共通するところなんだろうか… ③ いや　違う ④ 女子社員が特につめたいのだ　やはり　あの日のあの軽はずみな発言に原因がある ⑤ このパンは　あまりうまくないな　専門家を集めてもっとうまいパンのメニューを作ったらいいと思うな ⑥ 宣伝課の鈴鴨という女子社員まで何かよそよそしい ⑦ どうぞ ⑧ きっと俺の悪い噂はこの職場中の女の子の間に広まって鈴鴨もそのことを聞いた

My desktop is the clearest proof of all. Flowers are placed every day on the other managers' desks, but there isn't a single flower on mine.

①

Click!

Whew.
②

① 何よりも如実に物語っているのは机の上だ 他の課長の机には毎日花が置かれているのに俺の机の上には全然ない　② ふう

① ドルルル ②あ もしもし 奈美か お父さんだ ③うん…うん 元気だよ まだ起きてるのか？ ④実
はね お父さん またちょっと悩んでるんだ ⑤どうしたの 言ってごらん？ ⑥…うん…うん…ふーん

120

But it's easy! All you have to do is learn to like bread. You just have to get so you think the bread is delicious, right? ①

Oh, Mom. ③

It's Dad in Kyoto. ④

Wanna talk? ⑤

Nami! Who are you talking to? ②

Click ⑦

Mom says it's okay. Well, goodbye. ⑥

Learn to like bread, huh? I guess that makes sense. ⑨

Plunk

B-U-U-U-U ⑧

....

① 簡単じゃない パンを好きになればいいのよ そのパンがおいしいと思うようになればいいんじゃない？
② 奈美！ 誰と話してるの？ ③あ ママ ④京都のお父さんから ⑤出る？ ⑥ママ いいって！ じゃね！ ⑦ガチャ ⑧ツー ⑨パンを好きになれ…か なるほど

121

Kyoto Factory Slogan ①
Quality Improvement · Action Guidelines

In my old department, all we did was make commercials for products that had already been fully developed. We knew nothing about all the hard work that went on behind the scenes. ③

I get it now. The development of each new product begins with the kind of unsung effort demonstrated by those women and their recipes. ②

From now on I'm going to eat bread for lunch every day. Even if I never learn to like it, I'm going to keep eating it until I know the difference between good and bad bread. ④

That's the one and only way I can make amends for what I said. ⑤

① 伏見工場スローガン ② そうなんだ ひとつの商品を開発するのには そういう地道な努力から始まるんだ
③ 俺達は今まで出来あがった商品のCMを作る仕事しかしていなかった そういう陰に隠れた苦労を全く知らなかった… ④ これから昼食は毎日パンを食べよう 好きにはなれなくてもパンの良し悪しがわかるまでパンを食べつづけよう ⑤ それが俺の罪を贖う唯一つの方法なんだ

① 長い贖罪の日々だ　② こうやって　ひとつの製品が生みだされるんだ　その感触がだんだんわかってきた…　③ 今まで　こんなに真摯になったことはなかった…　④ ねえ　島課長　いつも昼食の時にいなくなるわね　どこに行ってるの？　⑤ 知らない　⑥ 俺はがんばるぞ　早く事業部の人間になりきるんだ!!

General Manager ①

Shun'ichi Kurashige, Director and General Manager of Electro-thermic Equipment Manufacturing ②

As you know, our breadmakers have become really popular in America, and a large group of business leaders from Chicago will be coming to visit soon. I want you to show them around a bit while they're here. ⑤

Yes, sir. ④

Shima, you can speak English, right? ③

Certainly, sir. ⑥

① 事業部長室　② 取締役　電熱器事業部事業部長　蔵重俊一　③ 島君　キミは英語が出来るんやったな！
④ はい　⑤ アメリカで　うっとこのパンメーカーがごっつう評判になりよってな…シカゴの経済団体のエライさんが近いうちにどっと来よるんや　そん時は案内役たのみたいんやが！　⑥ わかりました！

124

① それから夜は祇園へ連れてって接待してくれや　② 祇園？　お茶屋ですか　③ そや　これからこういうこともままあるので　キミも少しその方面に顔がきくようになっといた方がいい　④…そうやな　今晩ワシにつきおうてくれ　馴染みのお茶屋と女将を紹介しとくさかい　⑤ 島君は酒の方はいけるクチか？　⑥ はい　人並みに　⑦ オンナはどうや？　⑧ オンナはだめです　⑨ 本当に今は　とてもそんな気になれない

125

At present there are a number of entertainment districts in Kyoto, including Ponto-chō, Shimabara, Kamishichiken, Gion Higashi Shinchi, and Miyagawa-chō. But the most famous place of all is Gion Kōbu. There are about 120 teahouses here; it is a place where the "walk-in customers respectfully refused" rule is strictly observed.

①

What exactly is a teahouse? In short, it is a place where customers rent a private banquet room and entertain with food and drink. They summon geisha and maiko, and order in food from an outside caterer. That's all there is to it. Nonetheless, it's out of reach for the ordinary person.

②

① 京都は現在　先斗町　島原　上七軒　祇園東新地　宮川町などの花街があるが　最も有名なところが　ここ祇園甲部である　祇園甲部のお茶屋は約120軒　"一見さんお断り"の格式を厳として崩さないところだ　②では　お茶屋とは一体　いかなるものか？　一口で言えば　客が座敷を借りて酒食の遊びをするところである　そこに芸妓　舞妓を呼び　料理は別の仕出し屋から取り寄せる　ただ　それだけの場所だが　一般の人間には　なかなか敷居が高いのだ

That's right. In a way, it's similar to a members-only golf course. ②

I've heard it's absolutely impossible for a first-time customer to enter a teahouse in Gion Kōbu... ①

A guest can't play unless he's accompanied by a member. The club needs someone they can count on to take responsibility if the guest causes any trouble. ③

Actually, a person at my level can't normally come to this kind of a place, but because my old man was a carouser and a member... ④

Sa im on

...we've had admittance here for two generations, from father to son. ⑤

① 祇園甲部のお茶屋には　初めてのお客は絶対にあがれないと聞きましたが…　② そやな　ま　メンバー制のゴルフ場思うたらいい　③ ビジターだけじゃ遊べんけど　メンバーさんに同伴してもろたらOKや　トラブルがおきた時の責任を　はっきりとれる人間が必要なんや　④ ほんまは　ワシクラスのレベルの人間じゃ　こんなところに来れへんのやけどな…オヤジが遊び人でメンバーやったさかいな　⑤ 親子二代でこの店使わしてもろとるんや

127

① おかみ　新人連れて来たぞ　② ようおこしやした　西紋のフクどす　よろしゅうに　③ は　初めまして
島耕作と申します　④ 蔵重はんとは　もう30年以上もおつきあいさせてもろうとるんどすえ！　⑤ はあ
⑥ 不粋ですが　こういうところは初めてなので　今日は勉強させて下さい　⑦ よろしゅうおす　東京の人は
はっきりものゆうて気持ちがよろしいな

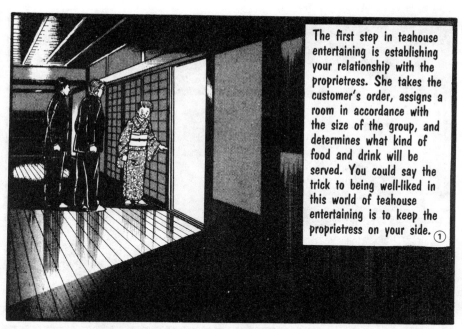

①お茶屋遊びの第一歩は　まずおかみとのつきあいから始まる　おかみは　客の注文を受け　人数に合わせて部屋を決め　酒肴のセッテイングをするポジションだ　このおかみをおさえておくことがこの世界でモテるコツだと言える　②部屋に通されると酒と簡単なつき出しが用意され　舞妓　芸妓が来るのを待つ　③今晩は　④舞妓は人数が少ないので　予約しておかなければまず座敷に呼ぶことは出来ない

The Mo-o-o-on—

Today, they called in not only a maiko but a dancing geisha and an accompanist. They danced "Gion Ballad" and "Even to the Plums Comes Spring" for us. ①

The banquet begins when the food arrives from the caterer. With the maiko and geisha pouring sake, we lost ourselves for a time in nonsensical banter. ②

They have much in common with Noh drama. You mustn't show sensuality in the dance. ⑤

In traditional Kyoto dancing, the local ballad dances are best, don't you agree? ④

Though we call them maiko, without their makeup they're just girls of about high-school age. So it's not as if they have a lot to talk about, but when talk turns to the world of dance or the theater, they are truly professionals. You can't keep up with just a superficial knowledge. ③

① 今日は舞妓の他に 立方の芸妓と地方の芸妓を呼んだ 「祇園小唄」「梅にも春」を舞ってもらう ②仕出し屋から料理が届けられたところで宴が始まる 舞妓 芸妓の酌を受け たわいもない戯言にしばし時を忘れるのだ ③ 舞妓といっても化粧をとれば高校生ぐらいの年齢の女の子だ たいして話題があるわけではないが 舞踊の世界や梨園の話題になると やはりプロフェショナルである なまじの知識ではついてゆけない ④ 京舞なら地唄舞がいちばんやな ⑤ 能に通じるとこがあるんどす 舞に色気を出したらあきまへん

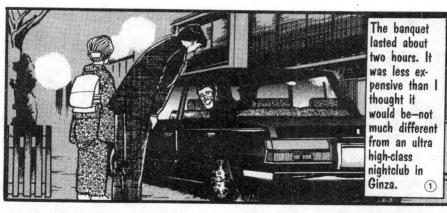

The banquet lasted about two hours. It was less expensive than I thought it would be—not much different from an ultra high-class nightclub in Ginza. ①

You must be tired. ③

Whew. ②

Vroom

You shouldn't be. Even though they don't know the etiquette, foreigners actually behave more appropriately than first-time Japanese. They don't go loosening their ties right away. ⑤

No, this was easy. I'm just concerned that when I come with foreign clients in the future, they might cause trouble because they don't know how to behave. ④

紋

Yow, she got me there. ⑦

Huh? ⑥

① 宴は大体２時間で終わる　費用は思ったよりも安く　銀座の超一流クラブと大差ない　② ふう　③ お疲れさんどす　④ いえ　まだ楽ですよ　これから外国人のお客をお連れすれば　いろいろなしきたりがわからないからご迷惑をかけそうで心配です　⑤ そんなことおへんで　外国の人は作法は知らなくても初めての日本人よりむしろ　お行儀は出来てはります　すぐネクタイゆるめたりはしまへんで　⑥ は　⑦ うへはやくも１本とられた

This is terrible! It's really coming down. ①

splash splash

Whew. Suddenly I'm exhausted. Humoring the general manager plus worrying about the customs of Gion... I'm worn out. ②

Darn! No matches. ④

I think I'll take shelter under these eaves for a minute. ③

①まいったな　すごい雨だ　②ふう　どっと疲れた　事業部長の相手に加えて　祇園のしきたりに気を遣って
くたくただ…　③少し　この軒で雨やどりをしていこう　④チェッ　マッチがないや

132

① マッチならこれをお使いやす　② また雨の日にお逢いしましたね　③ あ　あなた　あの時の！　④ そう
先日　都をどりの帰り道で傘にいれてもろうた女です　⑤　どうですか　今度は私の傘にはいりまへんか
⑥ は？　⑦ ここ私のお店なんですよ　⑧ そりゃいい考えだ

133

① うわ！　京都らしくていい店だ！　②おおきに！　水割りでよろしいか？　③はい！　④このあたりの飲み屋さんは大体会員制なんですか？　⑤半々でっしゃろか…私んとこは芸妓時代のお客はんがついててくれはりますんで少数の会員制でやってゆけるんです　⑥でも　おかげで雨なんか降ると店はこの通り…寂しいこと　⑦どうぞ

①へえ　ハツシバさんの方ですか　②そう　ハツシバでもいろいろあって　パンメーカーを作っている工場に勤務してます　③知ってる？　パンメーカー？　④知ってますよ　有名ですもん　⑤島耕作さん　いいお名前ね　⑥でもさ　就任そうそう工場の女子社員に総スカンくらって大変なんだ　⑦あら!?　どうして？　⑧彼女達が汗水流して作りあげたパンを事情も知らずに"まずい"なんて言っちまったんです　⑨まそれは大変…でどうなさったの？

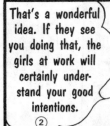 

That's a wonderful idea. If they see you doing that, the girls at work will certainly understand your good intentions. ②

First I decided I have to learn to like bread. So now I'm secretly eating nothing but bread every day. ①

It stopped raining. I'd best be on my way. ⑤

No, I don't want them to see me doing it. It's embarrassing to have other people see you struggling with something, don't you think? ③

Hee hee. It's so cute when men show their vanity. ④

Yes, I definitely will. ⑦

Please come again, okay? ⑥

① まず自分がパンを好きにならなきゃいけない…そう思って毎日こっそりパンばかり食ってます ② うん それとってもいい考え その姿を見たら会社の女の子たちもきっとわかってくれはるわ ③いや そんなところを見られるのはイヤなんだ なんか努力する姿を他人に見られるって恥ずかしいでしょう ④うふっ 男の人のそういう見栄って可愛いわ ⑤雨もあがったしそろそろ帰ります ⑥ね また来て下さいね ⑦はい

① 翌日　出社すると　② おはよう　③ おはようございます　④ 机の上に花が一輪　⑤ 鈴鴨君　この花は君
が…？　⑥ はい

① あ…有難う　② 姉がよろしくって言ってました　③ 誤解していてすみませんでした　④ え？　⑤ まさか
⑥ 会員制すず鴨　⑦ 先斗町　袖より合うも　春の夜の　他生の縁と　なつかしむなり　新村出

Don't Cry, Tanaka-kun!
Author & Artist: Hiroshi Tanaka

Essay by Mark Schilling

Who is this creature, the "salaryman"? The usual translations of this Japlish term—
"office worker," "white-collar worker," "businessman"—are serviceable enough, but
they don't begin to bridge the cultural divide between Japanese and Americans in
their perceptions of the salaryman phenomenon. To Americans who know the Japanese business world only from Michael Crichton's *Rising Sun* and newspaper stories
about *karōshi* (death from overwork), the typical Japanese businessman is a latter-
day kamikaze pilot in a blue suit who will willingly sacrifice family and self for the
corporate bottom line.

This stereotype, like all stereotypes, contains a grain of truth. Japan is full of
workaholics who come home only to sleep and have little more than a nodding
acquaintance with their families. There is even a folk saying that all that wives can
expect in the way of conversation from such types is *"Furo, meshi, neru!"* ("I want
a bath, food, and sleep!")

But there are also plenty of salarymen who don't fit the stereotype. During the
weekdays, when Japan Inc.'s workaholics are supposedly slaving away, movie the-
aters are filled with salarymen taking in the double feature, coffee houses are packed
with salarymen perusing manga, and quiet side streets are lined with parked company vans and cars, engines running and drivers snoring. In other words, an awful
lot of salarymen are doing an awful lot of goofing off. Even the ostensible
workaholics are often out partying after hours at a Taiwanese hostess bar—not
camping out next to the word processor.

The Japanese themselves are quite aware of this slacker side of their business life.
The bumbling, bone-lazy salaryman has long been a stock figure of comedy in the
mass media. National newspapers, including the sober-sided *Nihon Keizai Shimbun*,
Japan's leading business newspaper, run four-frame manga whose heroes are *hira
sarariiman* (rank-and-file office workers) of the hapless sort. The salaryman hero of
Diary of a Fishing Freak, a hugely popular film series based on a long-running
manga series by Jūzō Yamasaki, quite explicitly puts fishing ahead of his job.

Given these and similar pop culture depictions of salarymen, it's hardly surprising that the term itself has become something of a synonym for unambitious time-
server. Calling an upper-division sumo wrestler a *sarariiman rikishi* ("salaryman
wrestler") is not a compliment; it implies that his only goal in life is to get the minimum of wins needed to avoid demotion to the lower, unsalaried ranks.

The most unambitious salaryman of all, however, is probably Hiroshi Tanaka's Tanaka-kun. The hero of a popular manga that has been running in the monthly *Manga Life* since 1984, Tanaka-kun is a goof-off and screw-up extraordinaire, who doesn't have fishing as an excuse. He has his pride, but nothing to be really proud of, except a certain talent for dodging work—and most of the time his clever schemes turn into disasters. One day, he calls in sick to work and takes a skiing holiday, cleverly wearing a ski mask to avoid a telltale suntan. But as his colleagues notice with some bemusement when he hobbles in the next day, this "cold" sufferer has mysteriously acquired a pair of crutches.

Tanaka's boss is continually scolding him for such misdeeds and messes, and Tanaka is continually getting angry at his boss for treating him like an incompetent bungler. His ways of getting even are imaginative, to say the least: on one occasion, he sends his boss a case of cigarettes so that he can smoke himself to death; on a night out at a karaoke club, he croons insults when he thinks the boss isn't listening.

This streak of sneaky rebelliousness in no way implies that Tanaka-kun is a member of the so-called *shinjinrui*, the hip "new breed" of young Japanese who disdain the blind company loyalty and self-denying work ethic of their elders. Though young, Tanaka-kun is too hopelessly dweebish to ever be on the bold, cutting edge of anything. He is, in fact, something of a Japanese Dagwood Bumstead, a figure who remains stuck in the same ridiculous attitudes, year after year, decade after decade. But whereas Dagwood is forever running away from a screaming Mr. Dithers, Tanaka-kun is forever getting bopped on the head by a rock for yet another rock-headed stunt.

His creator, Hiroshi Tanaka, may be the one lobbing the rocks, but we also feel that he has an affection for his creation. One indication is the *kun* of Tanaka's name, an informal form of address that older men use with younger, usually in a fatherly or older-brotherly way. Tanaka may be a loser, but despite all the screw-ups and put-downs, he keeps bouncing back. Bitterness is not part of his nature; eternal optimism is. Also, despite his half-witted schemes for doing in the boss, he is not vindictive or mean. He is, in short, the salaryman as a fallible but essentially lovable human being.

Which, then, is the reality: the super-dedicated, super-efficient corporate warriors of Michael Crichton, or the amusing bumbler of Hiroshi Tanaka? Probably neither. For all the movie-watching, manga-reading and afternoon napping, the faxes get sent, the deals get done, the deadlines get met. Japan may no longer be regarded as the economic juggernaut and social paradise of bubble-era legend—years of recession and a few poison gas attacks have seen to that—but it still usually works. In this world, that's quite an accomplishment, and Japan's legions of salarymen are largely responsible for it.

A Sign of Repentance ①

The Diary ①

① 反省の色 ② おまえのミスが原因で仕事が大幅に遅
れちまったよ！バカモンが…③ 理容 ④ 責任をとって
頭をまるめたのか？だいぶ反省したよーだな…⑤ ハ
イ！⑥ これ…必要経費ですー ⑦ 散髪代？

① 日記 ② 何を書いてるの？ ③ 日記をつけてるんだ
よ。④ やーネー！日記というものは寝る前につける
ものよー。

The Man Who Skipped Work and Went Skiing ①

① 会社を休んでスキーに行った男 ② 田中さんカゼで休むそーです ③ …あやしいな〜 ④ スキーにでも行ってるんじゃないか？ ⑤ じゃ…雪焼けして帰って来るんじゃないですか ⑥ なるほど。雪焼けして会社に来てみろ…ただじゃおかんぞ〜 ⑦ ヤッホー！ ⑧ 雪焼けしないよーにマスクかぶってるんだもんネ！ ⑨ おっはよー ⑩ …やっぱり

The Substitute ①

Karaoke ①

① 代り ② 中田くんムリしないで帰りなさい。③ でも
これ今日中にやらないと… ④ あとは私がなんとかする
から早く帰ってカゼを治しなさい ⑤ はぁ…じゃ！そう
します ⑥ …というわけなんだ。田中くん彼と代ってく
れ！

① カラオケ ② ちぇっ…だれも聞いてない ③ 課長の
バカタレー　アホ　タコ　デベソー

143

Weak Points ①   Perm ①

① 弱味 ② 田中くん残業かわってくれない？ ③ えっ〜
④ おねがい！今日ちょっと用事があるの。 ⑤ ボクっ
て女性に弱いんだよな〜 ⑥ サンキュー！恩にきるわ
⑦ あれ？なにクソ…ん〜コノー…えい ⑧ キカイにも
弱いのね… ⑨ やっぱり私がやるわ

① パーマ ② トミ美容室 ③ ヘンなアタマになっちゃっ
たな〜… ④ 一夜明けてもやっぱりヘンだみんな笑う
だろーなー… ⑤ 田中くんは？ ⑥ アタマがヘンなの
で休むそうです

Fingernail Dirt ①　　The Man Who Felt Remorse ①

* The Japanese have a saying that if you drink tea made from the fingernail dirt of an esteemed individual, you will inherit that person's excellent qualities.

① ツメのあか ② 田中くんお茶！③ エラそーに…
④ ツメのあか入れてやる…⑤ おかしいなー　今日は
…ミスばっかりしてる　お茶を飲んでからどーもヘン
だ。

① 反省する男 ② あいつめまたパチンコに行ったな？
③ あのヤロー　帰ってきたらタダじゃおかんぞ。
④ すみませ～ん　もう二度とパチンコなんか行きま
せーん　カンベンしてくださ～い ⑤ そうとう負けた
な？

The Mentor ①   # The Goof-Off ①

① 先輩 ② 島田といいます　よろしくおねがいします ③ よろしくー　わかんないことがあったらボクたちにきいて!? ④ あのーこの書類なんですけどー…⑤ あっ…これネ！…これはネ… ⑥ たびたびすみません　この計算がわからないんですが…⑦ えーと…これはネ…⑧ あのーおトイレの

トイレットペーパーがきれたんですけど…どこに ⑨ ボクにはそんなのばっかりだネ…

① サボリマン ② よしよし ③ おまたせ致しました

146

Going Out ①　　　　　# A Man's Job ①

① 外出 ② 島田くん　ちょっと出かけてくるから…
③ ハイ！④ お帰りは何時頃に？⑤ ３時にはもどる
⑥ 島田さん　ちょっと外出してくるから… ⑦ ハイ
⑧ ２時30分にはもどります⑨ さぼるのネ

① 男の仕事 ② 田中くんちょっとお茶入れてくれ！
③ 課長！そういうのは女子にたのんでください!!④ 男
がお茶くみなんてできますか！男の仕事をさせてくだ
さい！⑤ よし！わかった⑥ おっとっと…⑦ がんばっ
てネー

The Man Who Screws Things Up ①

The Next Morning ①

① ミスをする男 ② あのーなにか仕事ありませんか？
③ キミは何をやらせてもミスするからなぁ〜 ④ この
手紙をポストに入れてきてくれ！これならさすがの
田中くんもミスはしないだろう。 ⑤ バカにして…
子供の使いじゃあるまいし…⑥ あっ！まちがえた…

① 翌朝 ② 毎日毎日チコクしやがってからに…もう許
さん 明日チコクしたらクビだー！ ③ ク…クビ？
④ 今日は会社に泊まっちゃお これなら安全だ…
⑤ 翌朝… ⑥ あっ！アパートの方に出勤しちゃった

148

Murderous Intent #1 ①

You're not good for anything. Why don't you go back to the countryside where you came from? ②

I can't let him get away with that. ③

I'll kill him! ④

Where did this come from? Hmm, I wonder how many more years I have to live... ⑥

100 YEAR CALENDAR ⑤

Heh heh heh

Murderous Intent #2 ①

You're completely worthless! A cat would be more help than you! ②

Section Chief

What does he mean, "A cat would be more help"?! I won't let him get away with that! ③

I'll kill him! ④

What is it?... A box full of cigarettes? ⑥

It's a gift from Mr. Tanaka. ⑤

CIGARETTES ⑦

① 殺意その1 ② 何をやらせてもダメだな―おまえは…田舎へ帰れ帰れ！③ 黙ってりゃいい気になって…もうカンベンしないぞ ④ 殺してやる。⑤ 100年カレンダー ⑥ だれだ？こんな所にこんなカレンダーを貼ったヤツは…ウ～ム…オレはあと何年生きられるのかな…

① 殺意その2 ② おまえは何の役にも立たん奴だな～ネコの方がまだましだ！③ ネコの方がましとはなんだ!! 絶対に許せない ④ 殺してやる。⑤ これ…田中さんからのお中元です。⑥ これ…全部タバコか？…⑦ たばこ

When I Graduate ①　　## Bonus Time ①

① 卒業したら ② 高校時代… ③ センコーめ　卒業したらぶんなぐってやる。④ 現在… ⑤ 課長めー　定年退職したらぶんなぐってやる。

① ボーナス ② ハイ！ごくろうさん。③ ありがとうございます ④ トイレでこっそり数えよっと！⑤ トイレ ⑥ 入ってます ⑦ こっちも… ⑧ こっちも…

Notes from the Frantic World of Sales

Author: Jirō Gyū   Artist: Yōsuke Kondo

Essay by Herbert Glazer

The hero of the story *Notes from the Frantic World of Sales* is a young employee of Tōa Electric, a fictional medium-sized manufacturer of electrical appliances. He is transferred to the sales department, where he is treated like a military recruit and discovers that the world of sales is a "battlefield." Even before the story shifts to the sales department, it is clear that there is a military influence in management, and military terms are used throughout this episode. The fighting, however, is between domestic makers—it's the story of how the smaller Tōa Electric successfully competes with giants such as Matsushita and Hitachi.

The victories (in this series, at least) are generally won through our hero's sincerity, goodness of heart, and willingness to give his all for his customers. To some American readers, this might seem like propaganda put out by company management to encourage their employees to be more loyal and dedicated, but in fact the setting is very familiar to the typical Japanese white-collar worker.

The introduction of the "military model" into the Japanese business world was the result of the business entrepreneurs of the early Meiji Period (1868–1912) consciously adopting the samurai ethic, due in part to the fact that many of them were actually former samurai themselves. They also were influenced by the pressure they felt to rationalize their motives for entering business and seeking monetary profits for their enterprises. They contrasted themselves with the merchant class of the preceding Edo (Tokugawa) Period (1603–1867); rejecting the unfavorable image of the Tokugawa merchant, whom they considered ignorant, vulgar, grasping, and immoral, they instead created a new image for themselves. They pictured themselves as the embodiment of the virtues of those who followed *bushidō* (the "way of the warrior") and the Confucian ethic. Their weapon was the abacus rather than the sword. It went beyond mere rhetoric: it was a totally new image.

Later in the Meiji Period, in the 1890s, labor unrest was countered by a number of new arguments which attempted to rationalize the working conditions of the era. The sweatshops of both the West and Japan had led to the introduction of factory legislation. In Japan this was opposed by the Meiji business community, who argued that Japanese industrial relations were qualitatively different from those of the West and that such legislation was not needed in Japan. They spoke of the uniqueness of the bond between Japanese employer and employee, governed by special feelings of affection and loyalty. The Tokyo Chamber of Commerce described the affection as essentially an extension of the sentiments that bound the Japanese family:

In our country, relations between employers and employees are just like those within a family. The young and old help one another and consult together in both good times and bad, and they are enveloped in a mist of affectionate feelings. . . .[1]

There are other contemporary references to the harmony, loyalty, and warm feelings between employer and employee. This same relationship was also referred to as "feudal," with the boss as lord and the worker as retainer. The Japanese boss (lord) treated his workers as if they were his own children. In response, the worker (retainer) not only performed his duties, in return for which he received the means for his sustenance, but he was also prepared, should circumstances demand, to give his life for his boss without hesitation or regret.

As Japan continued to industrialize, two distinct types of enterprise management evolved: *patriarchal* and *despotic*. Relationships between superior and subordinate in both systems were expressed through traditional Edo-period samurai class concepts of *on* (the incurring of obligations), *gimu* (the performance of duties), *giri* (a type of reciprocity in performance), and *ninjō* (human feelings which are suppressed when in conflict with *gimu*). Despotic systems arose as a result of the strain in the sense of mutual obligation between superior and subordinate.

Management and workers were likely to be suspicious of one another. . . . As a result authoritarianism grew. . . . The despotic employer . . . required a considerable staff of assistants, now to serve as a police corps rather than as a means of increasing his sensitivity to subordinates' needs. . . .[2]

It is therefore not surprising to recognize in the contrasting expectations of the young idealistic employee of this story and his authoritarian boss in the sales department echoes of the development of the Japanese industrial relations system. The younger man believes in the traditional idealized familial relationship between superior and subordinate that has been a fundamental component of the rhetoric enveloping the Japanese enterprise for more than a century. But instead, in his new assignment, he finds a harsh authoritarianism which has evolved as an inevitable consequence of the realities of the competitive capitalist environment of which the young employee is a part.

The typical Japanese recruit arrives at the company imbued with the idealism of his university days. He is then indoctrinated into a corporate culture that still has many of the trappings of feudal Japan with its emphasis on loyalty to the corporation. In other words, once he has been transferred from the relatively humane setting of General Affairs to the battlefield of Sales, our hero, Yōsuke Minamida, is a loyal samurai in the service of his despotic master—and he performs as such.

---

[1]Byron K. Marshall, *Capitalism and Nationalism in Prewar Japan—The Ideology of the Business Elite, 1868–1941* (Stanford: Stanford University Press, 1967), pp. 46–47.

[2]Solomon B. Levine, *Industrial Relations in Postwar Japan* (Urbana: University of Illinois Press, 1958), pp. 35–41.

Ordered to Duty in the Sales Division

営業部勤務を命ず

Tōa Electric Headquarters ①

Executive Office ②

You are being transferred from the Welfare Section of the General Affairs Department to Section 3 of the Sales Department. ⑤

Thank you very much. ⑥

Yōsuke Minamida! ③

Yes, sir! ④

<ruby>東亜電機本社<rt>とうあでんきほんしゃ</rt></ruby> ② <ruby>役員室<rt>やくいんしつ</rt></ruby> ③ <ruby>南田<rt>みなみだ</rt></ruby>ヨー<ruby>助<rt>すけ</rt></ruby>!! ④ ハイ!! ⑤ <ruby>総務部厚生課<rt>そうむぶこうせいか</rt></ruby>より<ruby>営業部第三課勤務<rt>えいぎょうぶだいさんかきんむ</rt></ruby>とする
⑥ どーも

154

...no matter where you look, the situation isn't pretty. ③

The development of new products, the improvement and expansion of our dealer networks, the stagnation of exports due to the high yen... ②

The electrical appliance industry is now in a free-for-all battle. You could say we have plunged into the equivalent of the Warring States period. ①

We face a time when each and every employee must throw himself into the battle like a human projectile. ④

In such times, I implore each of you to be all the more industrious and diligent. ⑥

Corporate wars are battles of intelligence and physical endurance. ⑤

① 電機業界は今や各社乱戦!! 戦国時代に突入したといっていい ② 新製品の開発　系列店舗の整備拡充
円高による輸出不振など ③ どれをとっても愉快な材料はない!! ④ これからはまさしく社員一人一人の
肉弾戦である ⑤ 企業戦争は知力と体力の戦いである!! ⑥ 各員一層の刻苦勉励を願いたいところである

① 本日より六名の者が新たに当営業三課に着任 ② おい自己紹介しろ ③ は　はい ④ ど－も厚生課から
きました… ⑤ やめい!! ⑥ 三課じゃいままでの社歴　職歴は一切無関係だ!! ⑦ は　はい!! ⑧ 南田ヨー
助です ⑨ 寺島敬治です ⑩ 春日井智生です ⑪ 高岸裕です ⑫ 鈴木健です ⑬ 河口仁です ⑭ いいか営
業という職場は得点主義だ ⑮ 野球でいうなら打撃力だ!! ⑯ 打率か打点かホームランだ!! ⑰ 守備は営業
の仕事じゃない!!

157

In that sense, there are no veterans or rookies! ③

The person whose bar graph is highest is the one who can walk tall in this company. ②

For Sales Department members, ability, pride, and status are all in the numbers. ①

TERAJIMA | NAKAYAMA | KITAMI | NOGUCHI | TAYAMA | MORIGUCHI | KAWAGUCHI | TEJIMA | TANAKA | K | MI | YAMADA ④

This morning's meeting is over! ⑧

We're wasting time. ⑦

Sell and sell and sell for all you're worth!! ⑥

SELL!! SELL!! ⑤

Yeah!! Sell!! One appliance sold is one appliance's worth of happiness!! ⑨

① 営業員にとって実力 誇り ステイタスはすべて数字だ!! ② 棒グラフが一番長い者が社内で肩で風切って歩けるんだぞ ③ その意味ではベテランも新人もない!! ④ 山田 宮 田中 手島 河口 森口 田山 野口 北見 中山寺島 ⑤ 売れよ!! 売れよ!! ⑥ 売って売って売りまくれ!! ⑦ 時間がもったいない ⑧ 本日の朝礼終わり!! ⑨ オスッ 売るぞ!! 一台売れば一台の幸福!!

① もしもし　こちら東亜電機ですが　② ワイワイ　③ おしておしまくれ!!　④ エッこれ以上手形サイトは短縮できませんよ　⑤ バーロ!!　⑥ 取引きをやめるっていうなら別ですがね　⑦ ガヤガヤ　⑧ ワイワイ　⑨ 販売店というのはダッコしてやりゃあ次はオンブしてくれっていうんだ　⑩ とても同じ東亜電機とは思えないなあ…　⑪ 始業時間前に朝礼　すぐさま実働とは…　⑫ じゃまだじゃまだ　⑬ わっ　⑭ ここは戦場だ…　⑮ ワイワイ　⑯ ナンダナンダ　⑰ ガヤガヤ　⑱ エッ!?　⑲ 課長が鬼軍曹で係長は伍長…　⑳ すると俺たちは二等兵かあ…

159

① その通りだ!! ② 南田に寺島は第三課第三係に配属だ ③ は はいッ ④ 俺が係長の柴田日吉丸だ よく
覚えとけよ ⑤ ガッチリ尻の穴から血が出るほど可愛がってやるからな ⑥ 辛くなったらいつでも夜逃げし
ていいぞ!! ⑦ 代わりはいくらでもいるからな ⑧ は はい! ⑨ よーしやすめ!! ⑩ ホッ

① 気_きをつけ!! ② 姿勢_{しせい}を正_{ただ}しくッ ネクタイはキチンと!! ③ 朝_{あさ} 歯_ははみがいたか? ④ は はい み みが
きました ⑤ よし 口臭_{こうしゅう}がしたんじゃ お得意_{とくい}さんに嫌_{きら}われる!! ⑥ いつもニコニコ清潔_{せいけつ}な人柄_{ひとがら}やさしい言葉_{ことば}
復唱_{ふくしょう}しろ!! ⑦ いつもニコニコ清潔_{せいけつ}な人柄_{ひとがら}やさしい言葉_{ことば} ⑧ そうだ それを「和顔愛語_{わがんあいご}」という ⑨ 和顔愛語_{わがんあいご}!?
⑩ 禅_{ぜん}の言葉_{ことば}だ ⑪ 休_{やす}め ⑫ 我_わが第三課_{だいさんか}の主力製品_{しゅりょくせいひん}は家電商品_{かでんしょうひん} 特_{とく}に冷蔵庫_{れいぞうこ} 洗濯機_{せんたくき}などの白_{しろ}ものだ ⑬ どう
やって一台_{いちだい}でも多_{おお}く市場_{しじょう}に送_{おく}りこみ ⑭ エンド・ユーザーの手_てに渡_{わた}すことができるか

Idiot!
How many years
has this company
been feeding
you?! ②

Uhh,
what are
"white goods"? ①

Huh?! ⑥

What do you
think selling
a product
entails?! ⑤

Let me
ask you
some-
thing. ④

"White goods" are things like refrigerators, washing machines, and dryers!!
It's an industry term that came into use because these items were originally painted white!! ③

You won't
sell a single
appliance on
our name!! ⑧

This
company isn't
Matsushita
or Hitachi. ⑦

Yeah? ⑪

To sell a product is to sell your own sincerity. Don't think you are selling refrigerators and washing machines!! ⑩

I'll tell
you this
just
once. ⑨

・・・・・・・・・

① あの～「白（しろ）もの」ってなんですか？ ② バカヤロー 会社（かいしゃ）で何年（なんねん）めし食（く）ってるんだ!! ③「白（しろ）もの」というのは冷蔵庫（れいぞうこ） 洗濯機（せんたくき） 乾燥機（かんそうき）などのことだ!! これらの商品（しょうひん）はもともと白（しろ）い塗装（とそう）がされていたところからついた業界用語（ぎょうかいようご）だ!! ④ 二人（ふたり）に質問（しつもん）する!! ⑤ ものを売（う）るとはどういうことか!? ⑥ エッ!? ⑦ うちは松下（まつした） 日立（ひたち）じゃねえんだよ 看板（かんばん）じゃ一台（いちだい）も売（う）れないぞ!! ⑨ 一度（いちど）だけ教（おし）える ⑩ ものを売（う）るとはこっちの誠意（せいい）を売（う）るんだ 冷蔵庫（れいぞうこ）や洗濯機（せんたくき）を売（う）ると思（おも）うな!! ⑪ はあ？

162

Sell your-selves! ①

Go sell your personality to the Moms and Pops of the retail shops!! ②

Yes, sir!! ③

Under-stand?! ⑤

Y–Yes, sir!! ⑥

It's no use mentioning the company's name and products until you've done that. ④

Even if the rounds are for introductions, go ahead and take lots of orders. ⑨

You have 25 shops each. Finish them in one week. ⑧

Each of you, make the rounds of your assigned shops and introduce yourselves. ⑦

That's the sales division for you—it has a portrait photo. ⑪

営業部第三課

南田ヨー助

東亜電機株式会社
東京都○○区○○町×丁目
電話○三五六×○×○×

These are your business cards. ⑩

① 自分を売るんだ　② 販売店のパパやママ　店員に自分という人間をトコトン売りこんでこい!!　③ はい!!
④ 会社の名前も商品もそれからじゃなきゃ役に立たんのだ　⑤ わかったか!!　⑥ は　はい!!　⑦ 各自担当店にあいさつ回りだ　⑧ それぞれ２５軒ずつ一週間ですませろ　⑨ あいさつ回り中であってもどんどん注文を取れ　⑩ これが名刺だ　⑪ さすが営業だなあ　顔写真入りだ

For your transportation expenses, go to accounting and get an advance. ②

Here's a list of your shops and a map of Tokyo. ①

THUNK

Under-stand?! ⑨

Anything you don't know, call in and ask! I will kindly and thoroughly teach you— even how to pee! ④

Don't forget to report back by phone while you're out! ③

Do this! ⑥

Do that! ⑤

When you get back to the office, write up a report! You're on your own! ⑧

No loafing along the way! ⑦

Aaaauuugh!! ⑩

But we have to do it... ⑬

Yeah. ⑭

Yeah. ⑫

Man, are we in trouble! ⑪

① これが店の名簿と都内の地図　② 交通費は経理にいって仮払いだ　③ 外からの連絡を忘れるな!!　④ 知らないことは電話してきけ!!　小便の仕方に至るまで親切ていねいに教えてやる!!　⑤ああしろ!!　⑥こうしろ!!　⑦途中でさぼったりするんじゃねえぞ!!　⑧ 帰社したら報告書の作成!!　つきそいは　なし!!　⑨わかったな!!　⑩ ガ～ン　⑪こりゃ大変だ…　⑫まったく　⑬でもやんなきゃ…　⑭まったく…

① わかったら各自担当店にあいさつ回りだ!!　② はい!!　③ あっ　④ あっ　⑤ 十円玉十円玉…　⑥ もたもたするな!!

① サブ～ ② とにかく当たって砕けろだ!! ③ やるっきゃない!! ④ レッツゴー!! ⑤ バーロー!! 急にとび
だしやがって!! ⑥ わっ ⑦ 企業戦線波高し…ここまでくれば進むしかない ヨー助は大丈夫なのだろうか

I'm #1!
Author & Artist: Kazuyoshi Torii

Essay by Bernice Cramer

When people hear that I spent thirteen years as a businesswoman in Japan, their first question is usually "How is that possible? I thought sex discrimination was the norm in Japan!" In fact, although foreign women (including me) are largely exempted from it, sex discrimination is still rampant in Japanese society. That's why the story of Ms. Asada, the automobile sales manager in the story *I'm #1!*, is so interesting.

Despite advances, it is still unusual to find a woman section chief in a Japanese corporation. So the shocked reaction of Kanetora Taxi's president upon learning that Asada is his salesman's boss is quite realistic. By the same token, the tough-minded Asada's unspoken reaction to his surprise—"I guess they're still around, this type"—seems to tell us more about the writer's fantasies than about the thought processes of Japanese professional women.

The manga is accurate in its portrayal of how professional women in Japan—especially those in sales—tend to capitalize on societal stereotypes. For example, Asada flirts mildly with Kanematsu, Kanetora Taxi's president, and he responds with a quite openly sexual reference. Clearly, she means to cultivate the customer's interest by whatever means necessary—even dirty talking. Later, Kanematsu wistfully mentions how nice it must be "to work with a beautiful woman." If these scenes had occurred in the United States, they may have been actionable under sexual harrassment codes.

Asada also resorts to shameless flattery, telling Kanematsu how impressed she is that he has built such a big business in only one generation. While salespeople the world over flatter their prospects, there is a clearly feminine tone to Asada's pitch, and the client falls for it completely. In an American business climate, Asada would be ostracized for using her gender so overtly to make a sale; in Japan, this is still quite common and even expected—especially in sales. Based on results, Asada's approach with customers is very successful. Fundamentally, it is those results which earned her the promotion to manager in the first place.

The manga is less realistic in its treatment of the dynamics inside a Japanese corporation, where, in fact, "sex-blind" support is extremely rare, and perhaps doesn't exist at all. In the beginning of the manga, the branch manager coolly orders Mr. Hikono to bring his superior, Asada, with him to the customer's office. Hikono is obviously discomfited by the situation, but the branch manager affects not to notice. This scene appears to evoke the writer's fears about what might happen once women become managers on a regular basis; perhaps this is a Japanese guess about the "dry" (or American-style) relationships that will be the norm between men and women colleagues in the next generation of business. Today, women managers are still a rarity and the boss would not have forced Hikono into such an embarrassing situation unless he was trying to teach him some kind of lesson. At a minimum, he would have acknowledged Hikono's discomfort.

Asada herself is unusual in the imperious tone she takes with Hikono, her male subordinate. Back in 1975, I remember meeting one of the very first Japanese women executives to become a board member of a publicly listed company. Her Japanese was very masculine and seemed to mimic the language of men in similar positions—an essential survival strategy in those days. Asada does not go that far; her Japanese is relatively feminine. However, she does seem to take pleasure in being snippy or rude to Hikono, and one almost senses a little Katherine Hepburn-style flirtation behind the attitude. This is not a typical relationship between manager and salesperson.

Also, compared to real-life business situations, Hikono seems a little too willing to learn from Asada. Japanese business is often highly political—an atmosphere partly fostered by the long tenure of well-entrenched employees—and my guess is that another man (not as nice—or perhaps, as smitten—as Hikono) would have rallied his cronies to fight back against his female rival, instead of appearing to knuckle under so readily.

Despite the retrograde picture I have painted of business relations between the sexes, things are changing in Japan. Of course, people in big, publicly listed companies tend to be more conservative, but there is now emerging a new generation of "gunslinging" women leaders at the helms of smaller, entrepreneurial companies. There are women in the Cabinet and the parliament of Japan, and women on the boards of directors of major corporations. There are even three publicly listed companies headed by women on the Tokyo Stock Exchange. While Asada is not quite believable now, she may well be a role model for the next generation.

R.POTENTIAL

The Lemon Secret

レモンの秘密

①そんないいかげんなセールスマンから車が買えるかッ!! ②おまえじゃ話にならん! 来るなら上司を連れてこいッ!! ③…フッ…確かに言われる通りだ…オレの慢心がこうさせたんだ… ④麻田課長を抜いてみせるなんて大笑いだぜハハ…

① 所長室　② 話はよくわかった　③ じゃあ所長に御一緒して頂けるんですかッ!?　④ いや、麻田課長と行
けッ！　⑤ ええッ…麻田課長とですか!?　⑥ なんだその顔は…麻田課長じゃ不服か？　⑦ い…いや、その…
⑧ キミの西地区担当を薦めたのは麻田課長なんだし…　⑨ やっぱり思った通り麻田課長の差し金だったか…
⑩ 販売市場（セールスマーケット）としては西地区はまったくの無風地帯…そこへこのオレをまんまと追い
やったワケだ…

① 実を言うとオレは西地区は現状維持がやっとで新規の開拓は難しいと判断したんだが… ② それを麻田課長は彦野クンなら可能性（ポテンシャル）を持ってるし必ず何かをやってくれる、と… ③ チェッ… 調子いいこと言って… ④ 初めのうちは一台も売れないかもしれないけど目をつぶってくれと頼まれちゃったよ。⑤ 相当キミのこと買ってるようだな、麻田クンは… ⑥ そ…そんな〜 ウソだろ… ⑦ もちろんオレだって麻田クンに負けないくらい買ってるんだぞッ！ ⑧ ハハ… ハイ… ⑨ おーし 頑張って行ってこいッ!! ⑩ ててッ

① んも～　麻田玲子がなに考えてるかますますわからなくなっちまった… ②ふう… ③どしたの？　サエない顔して… ④い、いえ別に…

No matter what, I just can't ask Section Chief Asada. I of all people... ①

The fact is, I challenged her, saying that I would outstrip her in sales. ②

Section Chief Asada!! ⑤

If I don't say it now, I'll never be able to. ④

But given the situation, I can't think about something like that... ③

Please!! Please go with me to Kanetora Taxi!! ⑥

①いくらなんでも麻田課長には頼めない… 仮にもオレは… ②彼女に対しセールスで抜いてみせると挑戦状を突きつけたんだ! ③…でもこの場合そんなことは… ④言いそびれるともう二度と言えなくなるぞ…! ⑤麻田課長…!! ⑥お願いします!! 金虎タクシーまで一緒に行って下さいッ!!

174

① 私に…？　②僕としては所長に頼んだんですけど…　③所長がどうしても麻田課長と行けって…　④ふうん…それで？　⑤客がどうしても上司を連れて来いってことで…その…　⑥あ、そう…　⑦ヘッ…あっさり断わられたか…　⑧やっぱり頼まなきゃよかった…

175

① 何してるのよ？ ② 金虎タクシーへ行くんでしょッ!? ③ 運転はあなたしてよ ④ 上着を早く着てきなさい ⑤ それで金虎タクシーは脈はあるの？ ⑥ …ハイ、あります

① タクシー　② …ふうん　ここね…　③ バムッ　④ こんにちは東京ワールドです!!　⑤ ありゃ？　また来やがった…　⑥ なんだ、女を連れて来たのか？　⑦ どうも初めまして　⑧ だ…誰が女を連れて来いと言った！　⑨ どうして上司を連れて来んのだッ!?

① 麻田と申します、ヨロシク ② なにッ か…課長!? ③ 女で課長なのか!? ④ まーまー座んなさい ⑤ いや〜 大したもんだ 女で課長、しかも美人ときてる ⑥ おホメを頂きありがとうございます ⑦ 女に「長」が付くとめずらしがる…まだまだいるのね こーゆー男… ⑧ あのー よろしかったらつまらない物ですがどうぞ ⑨ へ?

① レモン…？　② タクシーの運転手さんって朝までお仕事でお疲れでしょ？　③ どうしてもビタミンCが不可欠ですよね　④ さすが女は気がきくねえ～　⑤ でもなんか悪いなァ　⑥ 実を言うとパチンコでとったんですの　⑦ ええッ？　あんたもパチンコやんのかい？　⑧ 気分転換にはもってこいですわッ！　⑨ 意外だなァ　あんたを見た時はお高く気どったとっつきにくい女だなと思ったけど…ヘェ～

① セールスでなかなか車が売れない時など　面白くなくてついついパチンコを… ②やっぱ大変なんだ　セールスも…うん ③オレもパチンコは大好きなんだけどなかなか時間がなくて… ④でしょうね、社長サンはほんとお忙しそうですもの！ ⑤それに社長さんは拝見しただけでもバイタリテイのかたまりって感じですわあ ⑥いまでも週に10回はOK!! ⑦んまーパワフルですこと！

She's squirming...
③

It must have been that tenacity that allowed you to build such a splendid business.
②

hmph

hyuk hyuk hyuk

安全
迅速
意

Well, if I feel like it, even three times a day.
①

Huh? You mean you built up this taxi company in one generation?
⑥

I, Torajirō Kanematsu ...from the time I finished middle school until I established this company, did nothing but work—no playing around.
⑤

Clench

Yeah, back then it was so tough it almost did me in... No, really...
④

What in the world does a person do to succeed?
⑨

Mr. Kanematsu, by all means, please let me hear your story.
⑧

We have four branches now...
⑦

①まーその気になれば日に３回だって… ②会社をここまでご立派にされたのもその頑張りで… ③あせってる… ④う～ん、あの頃は死ぬほど辛かった…いやホントのハナシ… ⑤この金松虎次郎…今のこの会社を設立するまで中学出てから遊びもせず仕事一筋… ⑥ええッ？　じゃあ社長サンは一代でこのタクシー会社を!? ⑦まー今じゃなんとか営業所四か所… ⑧社長サン、是非ともお話を聞かせて下さい ⑨一体どうすれば成功するのかを…

The lemons, the pachinko, her speed in getting close to the customer... She really is good. ①

blah blah blah blah blah

And now, eagerly listening to someone's bragging that she doesn't want to hear at all... ②

How could the other person not be in good spirits? ④

Just like a mother, gently listening to a spoiled child jabbering away... ③

All of a sudden, I felt that I had caught a small glimpse into the true nature of our top salesperson, Reiko Asada. ⑤

KANETORA TA ⑥

① レモンといいパチンコといい、客の懐に入る素早さ…さすが巧い…！　② しかも聞きたくもない他人の自慢話を積極的に聞くなんて…　③ まるでだだっ子が一生懸命話すのをやさしく聞いてあげている母親のように…　④ 当然相手は気分の悪いはずがない…　⑤ この時オレは麻田玲子というトップセールスマンのほんの一端だろうけど本質をかい間見た気がした…　⑥ 金虎夕

① ほんとに今日はお忙しいところよいお話を聞かせて頂きありがとうございました　② なんだ、もう帰るんか？　③ いつまでもお邪魔するワケには…　④ いや〜、今日は久しぶりによく喋ったよ　⑤ 行くわよ　彦野クン　⑥ あ…あの〜課長ォ…　⑦ 仕事の話をしてくれなきゃ困るよう！　⑧ あ、それから社長サン　⑨ おー、なんだ？

① これからは我社の彦野が度々お邪魔すると思いますが　どうぞヨロシクお願いします　② か、課長…
③ おー！　あんたもたまには顔を見せろや　④ 食事おごるで…ちゃって　⑤ 来るなと言ってもお邪魔しますわ！　⑥ おー、又来いよッ！　⑦ じゃあ社長サン　頑張って下さい　⑧ ぎゅう　⑨ いいなあ若いの…美人と一緒に仕事が出来て　⑩ あ、ドーモ

① …課長ッ！　② どうして仕事の話をしてくれなかったんですか？　③ せっかく相手が気分よくしててチャンスでしたのに…　④ フッ…彦野クンなら当然気づいたと思ったけどナ…　⑤ 金虎社長が気分よくしてたからやめたのよ

① 言われる通り…気分よくさせておいてその直後に仕事の話をすればそれまでの会話はいかにも仕事がらみのお世辞にとられる… ② 逆に気分よくさせておいてスッと引き上げれば客に心地よい印象を残せるってことか…！ ③ やっぱり麻田玲子はすげえや！ オレなんかまだまだヒヨッコ、いやタマゴだぜ… ④ だからこそ麻田玲子に勝ちたい!! ⑤ こら～帰るぞ～ ⑥ 早くしてよ！ 鍵がないから入れないじゃないの～!! ⑦ すいませ～ん！ ⑧ 次の日…

186

Okay! I'm gonna make all those taxis our cars! ③

I'm Hikono from Tokyo World South!! ④

① 金虎タクシー　② 乗務員募集　③ よお～し！　あのタクシーを全部我社の車にしてやるぞ!!　④ こんちは～！　東京ワールド南の彦野ですッ!!

187

Salaryman Seminar
Author & Artist: Shōji Sadao

Essay by Steve Leeper

The Japanese love form. Whether they are serving tea or punches to the solar plexis, they want a teacher to show them exactly how it should be done (based on several centuries of refinement), and then they want to practice it until they get it exactly right. This attitude toward form extends to other aspects of life, like eating, being a man or a woman, and working for a company.

Not all Japanese follow the forms, of course. A few Japanese men do not start dinner every evening with a beer and a few Japanese women drive trucks. Exceptions are, to some extent, allowed, but everyone knows what the proper form is. And inevitably in a culture that values correct behavior over individuality, one fifty-year-old Japanese salaryman has a great deal in common with the next fifty-year-old salaryman.

The great beauty of such a society is its predictability; if you know what to expect, the daily activities of life become smooth and relatively effortless. The great weakness of such a society is its lack of versatility. Like people everywhere, the Japanese enjoy a certain level of novelty, but compared to Americans, the threshold at which novelty becomes incomprehensible, threatening chaos, is rather low.

The common theme in these selections from *Salaryman Seminar* is loss of predictability and the bewildering life of the average fifty-year-old salaryman. The problem is worse than a generation gap. Not only have the youngsters changed, they have diversified. Not only have they altered the forms, they are threatening the whole concept of form. They are worse than different—they are unpredictable.

So it is the threat to predictability that gives these selections their punch. Japanese readers laugh at these jokes because they feel the tensions described. American readers, I'm afraid, may not be even mildly tickled unless they: a) know the dominant patterns (the way things should be); b) recognize from their own experience the increasingly common exceptions described; and c) have some sort of emotional attachment to either the old or new patterns.

In the paragraphs below, I will offer some background information. Some of you may not require this information, and since there is nothing less funny than a joke explained, let me suggest that you abandon this introduction now and turn to the selections. Having read them, come back to read about the ones you didn't get.

• • • • • • • • •

Welcome back. I suspect you found the selection on page 190 self-explanatory. You might have laughed louder, though, if you had been physically hungry as a student and are now somewhat resentful of the rich kids you see around you.

The selection on page 192 depends on knowing that the vast majority of Japanese salarymen would consider half a bottle of certain expensive whiskies a genuine treasure. Even if they didn't drink, they would sense what the boss was up to and would play along. Here, the young guy inexplicably hates expensive whisky and unabashedly admits it, feeling free to frustrate and embarrass his boss.

The selection on page 194 is self-explanatory, but it might be helpful to know that discussions of sex are perfectly fine with the women you meet in hostess bars, while absolutely out of line with young girls entering the company.

To enjoy the selection on page 196 you need to know that a *neshōgatsu* (literally, "New Year's spent prone") is an accepted noun referring to a common pattern among tired, overworked salarymen who use their vacations for recovery. The fact that our hero can't find anyone else who slept the whole vacation is funny because it points to a profound change in attitude toward work as well as vacation.

The selection on page 198 is an obvious comment on the rising power of women. The wife's refusal to run across the street to buy some food is indicative of the modern woman's refusal to be quite so subservient. The convenience store across the street is also a big change, which adds to the punch.

The selection on page 200 relies on the reader's knowledge about: a) the father's central, dominating role in the family; b) the way that role is changing; c) the very common experience of *tanshinfunin* (father transferred and living alone); and d) the well-known loss of regard suffered by fathers who spend too much time at work. Though fathers are still supposed to be central, governing authorities, they are now often irrelevant except as sources of income.

The hero of the selection on page 202 is a common type in Japan, one who makes a career out of knowing more about food and restaurants than anyone else. Usually such people are high-ranking executives with plenty of chances to travel and entertain at the company's expense. The rest of the guys are eager to learn from their more sophisticated colleagues. However, the really sophisticated ones these days are the young women with the time and money to go overseas during every vacation.

Though you undoubtedly understood that lack of respect for hierarchy is the focus of the selection on page 204, you probably did not laugh unless you could actually feel the frustration of the guy in the sand who, being in his late thirties or early forties, genuinely wants nothing more than to jump up and bow low.

The selection on page 206 drives to the heart of the problem. The young ones don't care: they don't care about the *bōnenkai* ("end-of-year party") tradition, about the food or entertainment, or, worst of all, about the older guys and the group as a whole. People who don't care are utterly unpredictable and impossible to relate to.

The selection on page 208 takes the lack of caring to its ultimate conclusion. To avoid embarrassment, and perhaps being controlled by others, the young ones will even drop out—an unthinkable alternative for their elders.

Salaryman Seminar

For a student job, it's not so bad. ③

It must be rough, this job. ②

Part-time worker ①

Well! I'll have to take you out one night. My treat. ⑥

That's my alma mater! ⑤

What's that? M University? ④

Actually, I'm just working to get money for a trip to Hawaii. ⑧

Housing is expensive these days. It must be hard for students. ⑦

① バイト君 ② 大変だろ　この仕事も ③ 学生のバイトとしたらラクなほうです ④ ナニ？　M大？ ⑤ じゃ
オレの後輩じゃないか ⑥ オーシこんどおごってやろう ⑦ いまは下宿代も高いから学生も大変だよなァ
⑧ いや　ハワイへ行く資金かせいでるんです

⑨ハワイ!? ⑩もう三度めなんスけど ⑪三度め!! ⑫オレなんかまだいっぺんも ⑬ボク　クルマですので このへんで ⑭ごちそうさまでした

Salaryman *Seminar*

Here we have one bottle of liquor. It contains exactly one-half its capacity. ②

POSITIVE PEOPLE MAKE COMPANIES GROW ①

This is great stuff! ④

Do you think the bottle is half full or half empty? Those who think it's half full are positive people. ③

The contents are exactly one-half. ⑥

This is half a bottle of liquor. ⑤

①積極人間が会社を伸ばす　②ここに一本の酒がある。中身はちょうど半分である。　③これを「もう半分しかない」と思うか「まだ半分もある」と思うか。「まだ…」と思う人が積極人間である。　④いーこと書いてある　⑤ここに一本の酒がある　⑥中身はちょうど半分だ

192

⑦ ところでキミはこんないい酒のんだことある？　⑧ ありません　⑨ それはかえって都合がいい　そこで聞こう　⑩ 「もう半分しかない」と思うかね？　それとも「まだ半分もある」と思うかね？　⑪ さあどっちだ？　⑫ どっちでもありません　⑬ ボク酒は大きらいですから　⑭ なんとも思いません

Salaryman Seminar

It really hurt a lot, and it wasn't good at all. ④

When I was 18. ③

So, when did you lose your virginity? ②

CLUB RAMERU ①

New Employee Welcoming Party ⑤

① CLUBらめーる ② で ロストバージンはいつかね？ ③ 十八のとき ④ 痛くて痛くてなーんもいいことなかった ⑤ 新入社員歓迎会

⑥ 新入女子社員　⑦ で　ロストバージンはいつかね？　⑧ ン？　⑨ 課長っ!!　⑩ いや　わたしとしたことが つい口がすべって　⑪ 時と場所もわきまえず…　⑫ 十七のときでした　⑬ 高校の五年先輩で海の見えるシティホテルでした　⑭ で二人めが…

Salaryman Seminar

① ヨォ ② 正月はどっか行ったの？ ③ ええ ④ 南フランスのほうをまわってきました ⑤ おもしろくない
⑥ まわるゥ… ⑦ 正月はどっか行ったの？ ⑧ ええ ⑨ アカプルコとか行ってきました ⑩ おもしろくない
⑪ とかァ…

⑫ 正月はどっか行ったのかい？　⑬ 寝正月でした　⑭ そう！　⑮ 正月は寝正月にかぎるッ　正月海外行くやつバカ　⑯ タヒチの海辺で正月中ずっと寝てました

Salaryman Seminar

① ヨーシおれんちでのみなおそう　② カーチャンただいま　③ ウィスキー持ってきてねー

④ ツマミはどうした　⑤ あいにく冷蔵庫がカラで　⑥ つべこべ言わずに買ってこーい　⑦ いま何時だと思ってんですか　⑧ どこかやってるとこあるんですか？　⑨ ハイマート　⑩ マート

Salaryman Seminar

Hey, I just remembered! Tomorrow is Father's Day! ④

On solitary assignment away from home ③

The 3rd Saturday in June. ①

If I catch the 6AM train... I can be home by 10. ⑥

I'll get up early and make the trip home. ⑤

① 土　② 六月第三土曜日　③ 単身赴任　④ そうだ　あしたは父の日だ!!　⑤ 朝早く起きて帰ってやるか
⑥ 朝六時の列車にのれば十時にはウチにつくな

⑦ ただいま ⑧ アラ帰ってきたの ⑨ わるいけどわたしきょう鎌倉彫りの日だから帰りおそくなるわよ
⑩ あたしもテニスでおそくなるわよ ⑪ ボクは部活 ⑫ みんな父の日を ⑬ 忘れてるッ

Salaryman Seminar

It's very popular these days, you know. ③

What? You two don't know about ethnic food? ②

Gourmet Section Chief ①

I'm crazy about the stuff. ⑥

There's Mexican, Cambodian, Sri Lankan... ⑤

Well, let's see, in a word, you could also call it ethnic "cuisine." ④

Yeah! Mexican food! ⑨

That is some unusual food. ⑧

The other day I went out for Mexican. ⑦

① グルメ課長　② なんだキミラ　エスニック料理も知らんのか？　③ いま　はやってるんだぜ　④ ま　ひとくちにいうと民族料理とでもいうのかナ　⑤　メキシコ料理とかカンボジア料理とかスリランカ料理とか　⑥ ボクはいまそれにこっててね　⑦ こないだはネ　メキシコ料理食べてきたヨ　⑧ これがまた変わっててね　⑨ 知ってる！　メキシコ料理！

⑩ オー！　知ってるかメキシコ料理！　⑪ こりゃ話が合うナ　⑫ 渋谷のホラ！　道玄坂のウラのほうへ行った店だろ!?　⑬ イーエ　⑭ メキシコの現地で　⑮ スリランカ料理も現地で　⑯ こりゃ話が合わんなァ

Salaryman Seminar

Hmph. ②

Department Head ③

COMPANY BEACHHOUSE ①

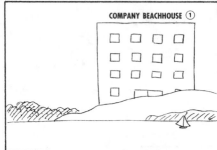

If you pass each other in the hallway, you ought to at the very least exchange greetings. ⑤

The young ones these days have no manners. ④

① OOKK海の家　② ウオッホン　③ 部長　④ 近ごろの若いもんは礼儀をしらん　⑤ 廊下ですれちがったらあいさつぐらいするもんだ

⑥会社も海の家も同じなんだよ　⑦ッタクモー　⑧ブツブツ　⑨アッ部長　⑩キミーッ　⑪寝たままであい
さつしていいのかッ　⑫ドモドモ

Salaryman Seminar

① 忘年会にあたって新人類のキミらの意見もきいておこうと思ってね　② 会場についての注文は？　③ 別に
④ 食べ物や飲み物についての希望は？　⑤ 特に　⑥ カラオケなんかあったほうがいいかね？　⑦ どうでも
⑧ はりあいのない奴らだなァ　⑨ 忘年会会場

"Old generation" ⑩

So this is why they said "not really," "nothing in particular," and "whatever"... ⑪

Cassette player ⑭

Chewing gum ⑬

Comic book ⑫

⑩旧人類　⑪これじゃ「別に」「特に」「どうでも」のわけだなァ　⑫マンガ　⑬ガム　⑭カセット

Salaryman Seminar

① 新人類　② 二十六日は課の忘年会よ　③ エーッ!?　④ なんか隠し芸を考えといたほうがいいわよ　⑤ エーッ!?
⑥ とくに新入社員は隠し芸とカラオケの両方をやらされるわよ　⑦ エエーッ!?　⑧ ボク人前に出るとあがっちゃってなんにもできなくなっちゃうんです　⑨ ドーシヨー　⑩ あのボクだけ除外してもらうわけにいかないでしょうか　⑪ そんなことできるわけないでしょ

208

⑫ そうだ!! ⑬ ひとつだけ隠し芸やらないですむ方法があった！ ⑭ いままでどうしてこんないい方法を思いつかなかったんだろ ⑮ アラ！ 新井クンどうしたの？ ⑯ さっき会社辞めたんです ⑰ いーなー

IF YOU LIKED *BRINGING HOME THE SUSHI*... YOU'LL LOVE *MANGAJIN* MAGAZINE!

Using the same authentic Japanese manga presented in *Bringing Home the Sushi*, *Mangajin* gives you an easy, entertaining way to learn Japanese and get a slice-of-life view of Japanese society at the same time.

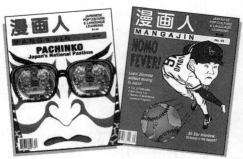

Over the past five years, *Mangajin* has become established as the magazine for people who want to get an inside look at Japanese language and culture—a view which is simply unavailable anywhere else.

Mangajin uses translations of authentic manga, the famous comics read by millions of Japanese daily, to take you inside a world few non-Japanese ever get to see.

Each issue features translations of excerpts from popular manga, carefully selected to reflect a cross-section of Japanese life and cover a wide range of language levels.

By providing a window into Japanese life, *Mangajin* makes the task of breaking through Japan's language and culture barrier less daunting. A single manga frame can capture an entire situation—language, gestures, etiquette and cultural nuance—like no ordinary textbook can.

But *Mangajin* is more than just manga. Every issue is packed with information on Japan: feature stories, articles and columns, political cartoons, basic Japanese lessons, and a classified section.

Get inside the *real* Japan. Call or fax and subscribe to *Mangajin* today!

Mangajin's manga translations take you inside the real Japan...

Here is how *Section Chief Shima*, from page 125 of *Bringing Home the Sushi*, appeared in *Mangajin* magazine. Along with the direct translation, *Mangajin* provides notes giving you valuable insights into both Japanese language and culture.

Mangajin's unique four-line translation format was created to reflect the linguistic logic of Japanese

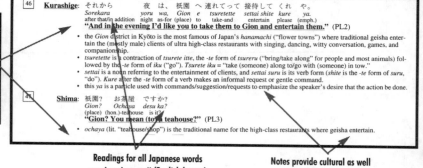

46 **Kurashige:** それから 夜 は、祇園 へ 連れてって 接待して くれ や。
Sorekara yoru wa, Gion e tsuretette settai shite kure ya.
after that/in addition night as-for (place) to take-and entertain please (emph.)
"And in the evening I'd like you to take them to Gion and entertain them." (PL2)

- the *Gion* district in Kyōto is the most famous of Japan's *hanamachi* ("flower towns") where traditional geisha entertain the (mostly male) clients of ultra high-class restaurants with singing, dancing, witty conversation, games, and companionship.
- *tsuretette* is a contraction of *tsurete itte*, the *-te* form of *tsureru* ("bring/take along" for people and most animals) followed by the *-te* form of *iku* ("go"). *Tsurete iku* = "take (someone) along to/go with (someone) in tow."
- *settai* is a noun referring to the entertainment of clients, and *settai suru* is its verb form (*shite* is the *-te* form of *suru*, "do"). *Kure* after the *-te* form of a verb makes an informal request or gentle command.
- this *ya* is a particle used with commands/suggestion/requests to emphasize the speaker's desire that the action be done.

47 **Shima:** 祇園? お茶屋 ですか?
Gion? Ochaya desu ka?
(place) (hon.)-teahouse is it'a
"Gion? You mean (to) a teahouse?" (PL3)

- *ochaya* (lit. "teahouse/shop") is the traditional name for the high-class restaurants where geisha entertain.

Readings for all Japanese words are given in romaji (English letters).

Notes provide cultural as well as linguistic background

Mangajin gives you insights into what's going on in Japan...

Mangajin is more than just manga. Each issue our reporters give you insights to into hot topics and current trends in Japan, like:

- Late-Night TV
- The Karaoke Craze
- Japan's Car Culture
- Eating on the Run
- Gambling in Japan
- Nomo Fever
- Japanese Beer Update
- Pachinko
- Sake Connoisseur's Guide
- Foreigners in Manga
- Japanese Pop Music
- Traveling in Japan

Mangajin brings you the latest on books, computers, and more...

With some of the world's sharpest Japan experts writing in its pages, *Mangajin* is your best source of information on Japan.

Whether you use a Mac or PC, our computer reviews keep you up-to-date on the latest in Japanese language-learning software, and also help you keep your machine computing fluently in Japanese.

You'll also find other features like political cartoons, product news, language bloopers and a column on Japanese cuisine.

Mangajin even provides a *Basic Japanese* column. Each "lesson" dissects and explains one specific concept of basic Japanese—a phrase, word, or hard-to-grasp idiom.

What the experts are saying about *Mangajin*...

"*Foreigners can master colloquial Japanese by reading **Mangajin** magazine...*"
—**The Wall Street Journal**

"***Mangajin** is...useful not only to Japanese language students, but to those who just want to get a peek behind the curtain and see what's really going on in Japanese society.*"
—**The Japan Times**

"***Mangajin** is an educational and thoroughly entertaining way to keep up with modern Japan.*"
—**T.R. Reid, The Washington Post**

"***Mangajin** can help Americans in any field, by teaching them something about the competition.*"
—**The Atlanta Business Chronicle**